MAKE PEACE WITH ANYONE

MAKE PEACE WITH ANYONE

BREAKTHROUGH STRATEGIES TO QUICKLY END ANY CONFLICT, FEUD, OR ESTRANGEMENT

DAVID J. LIEBERMAN, Ph.D.

ST. MARTIN'S PRESS ❦ NEW YORK

www.stmartins.com

ISBN 0-312-28154-4

10 9 8 7 6 5 4 3 2

CONTENTS

PART ONE
THE CAUSE OF ALL ARGUMENTS, CONFLICTS, FEUDS, AND ESTRANGEMENTS

PART TWO
THE SOLUTION TO ALL ARGUMENTS, CONFLICTS, FEUDS, AND ESTRANGEMENTS . . . WITH REAL-WORLD, REAL-LIFE EXAMPLES AND SCENARIOS

SECTION I: KEEPING SPARKS FROM BECOMING FLAMES: PUT OUT THE FIRE BEFORE IT EVEN BEGINS BY HANDLING DIFFICULT PEOPLE, CONVERSATIONS, AND SITUATIONS THE BEST WAY, RIGHT AWAY

ACKNOWLEDGMENTS

It is a great pleasure and privilege to acknowledge the tremendous work of the outstanding professionals at St. Martin's Press. Many thanks to my editor, Jennifer Enderlin, for her keen insights, ideas, and dedication to this book. And to the talented people in the production, publicity, marketing, advertising, art, and sales departments a warm and genuine thank you: Sally Richardson, Matthew Baldacci, Alison Lazarus, John Cunningham, John Murphy, John Karle, Mike Storrings, Janet Wagner, Mark Kohut, Darin Keesler, Lynn Kovach, Jeffrey Capshew, and Ken Holland. And my thanks to the entire Broadway Sales Department for their continued and tireless efforts on behalf of this book.

This book benefits tremendously from having been reviewed in its earlier stages by Rabbi Aryeh Leib Nivin of Betar Illit, Israel. Moral judgment calls for acceptable strategies are pivotal to making peace. Rabbi Nivin's wisdom and thoughtful insights are integrated throughout this text. And anything that may appear to be a deviation from a higher moral ground should in no way be considered a reflection of his contributions but rather a departure to effectively illustrate a point.

Thank you to my friends and agents Michael Larsen and Elizabeth Pomada, two of the kindest and finest people I have the pleasure to know.

And to those who recognize the importance and necessity of quality and healthy relationships, who strive, in the face of adversity, to make peace, this book is for you. May your pursuit be swift and rewarding.

INTRODUCTION

This book will teach you the greatest psychological secrets to end *any* argument, conflict, feud, or estrangement at home or in the workplace. If you're tired of all the anxiety, uneasiness, stress, and turmoil from a family feud, workplace disagreement, or personality conflict, then arm yourself with the techniques that bring people together, put differences in the past, and create harmony from discord.

This book shows you *step-by-step* exactly what to say and what to do to bring peace to any situation. Whether it's been ten minutes, ten days, or ten years, you can use the power of psychology to make any situation right.

This book is packed with powerful psychological techniques and tools, so you won't waste a second on philosophies, vague theories, or ideologies. We won't talk incessantly about the power of forgiveness or prattle on endlessly with cute stories that go nowhere and anecdotes from famous dead people. Yes, when you are angry you're only hurting yourself. *Of course.* But the real question is, then what?

This book shows you how to get the other person—or the two other people, if you're a third party—to move past the hurt, the anger, and the pain and *agree to make peace.* More than that, you will learn how to solidify the relationship—to create a stronger bond—so that you can keep similar problems from occurring in the future.

When you are done reading this book, you will be able to apply the techniques *as soon as you want.* There is no homework for you to do—no journals to fill out, no meditations about your feelings, and no additional reading

You will also see that throughout the book all the strategies are followed by specific examples to effectively illustrate the points and show you *exactly* how to apply the techniques. Just look for the "Real-

World, Real Life Example and Scenario" phrase for in-depth clarification of any psychological concept.

Now, as they say, the proof is in the pudding. And for that reason the "proof" isn't buried obscurely in the middle of the book. All the psychological strategies are written and structured to work independently, so you only have to learn what to do in your specific circumstance. The techniques are also scripted out so that you know *exactly* what to say and when and how to say it. You simply plug in the technique for your particular situation and you're done. So if time is of the essence or you just want to get things moving *now*, then simply go to the Contents, look up your situation, and follow the psychological strategy.

The power to end any argument, conflict, feud, or estrangement is now *yours*.

PLEASE NOTE
Throughout all the examples in this book the pronouns *he* and *she* are used alternately. This is done to make the language less sexist, not to indicate that one sex is more likely to be engaged in a certain type of conflict than the other.

WHAT THIS BOOK CAN DO FOR YOU

If you want to keep a difference of opinion from escalating into an argument, or give criticism without causing hurt feelings, you will learn the psychological secrets to deal with *any* difficult person, situation, or conversation, easily, calmly, and quickly.

&

If you're arguing over the same old things time and again, you can now get anyone to see and agree—*happily!*—with *your* point of view within minutes. In any relationship or situation, you can eliminate all those annoying quarrels once and for all.

&

And for those times when it's not a matter of what's right, fair, or just, and it's everybody for himself, learn the psychological secrets to quickly settle any conflict or deadlock *to your advantage.* Regardless of the circumstance, all conflicts come down to pure psychology, and these tactics will help you to come out the winner time and again.

&

Of course, since nobody is perfect, you can, in minutes, erase in the mind of anyone anything you said or did that caused embarrassment, resentment, or hurt feelings. When you are misunderstood, misspeak, or act without thinking, then use these psychological strategies to put out the fire *before* it even begins.

&

Most significantly, when you've done something that is clearly and objectively wrong—cheated, lied, stolen—and the situation seems hopeless, you can get things back on track, fast, no matter what you did or how much time has passed. If you truly regret your behavior, then get anyone to forgive you *and* learn how to reestablish trust faster and easier than you'd think.

&

Finally, and best of all, *you* can be the great peacemaker and make things *good again*! In any situation where there is an ongoing feud or longtime estrangement, you can intervene and bring peace now. In any relationship or situation—professional or personal—no matter how bad things are, you can bring people back together more quickly and easily then you ever thought possible.

IT'S GOOD TO KNOW
This book is divided into chapters offering specific psychological strategies. You may find, though, that techniques given in several chapters will also be effective in your specific circumstance. So to round out and improve your overall strategy to success, look at other chapters that may relate to your situation.

A NOTE TO READERS

The techniques and psychological strategies offered in this book can help you to create and reestablish enhanced and rewarding relationships. *There is one caveat.* I strongly encourage you to ask yourself the following question before using any of these techniques: "What are my motives?"

The reason is simple. If your intentions are selfish and manipulative, not only will you *not* be successful in achieving your objective—though it may appear that you have in the short term—but you may be causing yourself harm. I do not say this lightly. Why is this so?

Based on numerous studies and research in the area of relationships and psychological health, it has been clearly shown that your *motives* for reestablishing any relationship *must* be well intentioned and to the *mutual* benefit of all parties involved.

If this is not the case, you pay a big psychological price. The consequences are well grounded in several psychological principles that demonstrate clearly, no matter how they are rationalized and justified, that actions take a great toll on the psyche. Unconscious guilt eats away at your self-esteem and causes you to be less emotionally centered and stable, leading to an array of self-destructive behaviors.

The techniques outlined in this book will enhance your life and give you the opportunity to make things good when they go bad—the proverbial second chance. But again I caution that just because you *can* make things right, unless all persons involved gain, you will have achieved a short-term objective at a high long-term price.

XVI • A NOTE TO READERS

There are three main themes to the strategies in this book. Any techniques that encourage an expression of respect and actions that *strengthen* the relationship can and should be used liberally. Those techniques that require minor deception or exaggeration in order to save someone from embarrassment or hurt feelings should be used only when necessary in order to keep or make peace. Finally, any strategies that call for the use of psychological tactics to accelerate the peacemaking process should be used only *when* absolutely necessary, and you should use only *what* is exactly necessary. *Use what you need but only what you need.*

Trust, honesty, and respect are the building blocks of any relationship. The greater good should always be sought, the benefit to all parties should be clear, and your intentions should be sincere and honorable before applying any of these strategies.

And with that . . . let us begin.

PART ONE

THE CAUSE OF ALL ARGUMENTS, CONFLICTS, FEUDS, AND ESTRANGEMENTS

CHAPTER 1

How It All Begins

Why Do You Care if Someone "Gives You the Finger"?

What does it mean when we say that we are hurt? Or that someone has offended or embarrassed us? What do we mean when we say that something is unforgivable or that someone was rude or disrespectful?

What we are saying, simply, is that someone else's behavior caused us an emotional pain. Okay, fine. But this begs the larger question of *why* we are pained by these situations. Why do we even care? To say that we are hurt is not enough. To fully understand what is going on we have to answer the question *Why?*

Why Don't You Like Being Told to Shut Up?

Does it bother you when another driver cuts you off on the road? Or when someone rejects, ignores, or embarrasses you? Or for that matter steals, lies to you, or cheats on you? Of course you are left feeling hurt, betrayed, and angry, but the question is *why?* To say that you were treated contemptuously and disrespectfully is accurate, but why does that bother us?

Do you understand the larger questions here? Why does it pain us to be disrespected? Why do you care if someone gives you "the finger"? You don't bleed. It doesn't cost you anything. And you're not prevented from living your life. Yet it matters, and sometimes it matters a lot. So let's find out why we care.

CAN YOU TELL ME *SIMPLY* WHAT EXACTLY SELF-ESTEEM IS?

So often we throw around words like ego, self-esteem, fear, respect, anger, and projection. But what do they all mean, and more important, how are they all connected? Let's see exactly how, on a practical, everyday level, these words shape the way we see ourselves and impact on how we interact with our world. In a nutshell, let's look "behind the scenes" into the human mind.

In order to be happy, have good relationships, and be psychologically balanced, a person has to *feel good* about himself. This means that we need to literally *love ourselves*. And this self-love is called *self-esteem*.

Now, many folks insist that all we need to feel good about ourselves is to get a good dose of self-esteem, as if we could order it off the menu at Denny's. That would be great if we could, but self-esteem is a *by-product* of how you live your life. It cannot be gained directly. *It can be gained only through self-respect*. Why is this so? Simply, if you do not respect yourself, then you cannot love yourself.

HOW DOES A PERSON GAIN SELF-RESPECT?

We all make choices as we go through our daily lives. When we *choose* to do what we believe is the "right thing," we feel good about ourselves, and when we do what we know is wrong, we often feel guilt, embarrassment, and shame. These emotions tear away at our self-respect and eat away at our self-esteem.

Good enough. But what does this have to do with ending feuds and conflicts? We're getting warm. Because herein lies the basis for every type of interpersonal conflict.

Notice that we say *choose* to do what is right. In order to choose, you must be independent, meaning that you must be able to exercise your free will and not be *forced* to do the right thing. This is why any situation that robs us of our freedom in effect harms our self-esteem, because when our freedom is restricted our ability to *choose* is as well. Therefore we find that our sense of independence and self-esteem are intertwined. *And that's the key.* As we will see, it is the loss of independence that sparks all the conflicts you have—and holds the secret to resolving them effortlessly.

But let's back up for just a moment. When you make a decision in life, any decision, there is always one or a combination of three underlying motivations.

- You can choose what *feels* good.
- You can choose what makes you *look* good.
- You can choose to do what *is good* or right.

The first two motivations chip away at our self-esteem, while the third makes us feel good about ourselves and who we are. Let's take a look at how and why this happens.

When you choose to do something merely because it *feels good*—even though you know that it may be wrong—it robs you of your self-control. Your actions are dictated by *habits* and *impulses.* For instance, when you overeat, you don't feel good about yourself, and afterward you may even feel guilty and angry. Or if you sleep late when you had wanted to get an early start, you may become annoyed with yourself. When you make a decision that goes against your true inner desires—in this case to eat well or get up early—you are in effect a slave to your cravings. Hence, you are not free and not independent.

Now, when you do something merely because it makes you *look good* but you know it is wrong, you are not living for yourself but only for an image. When you are driven by this motivation, you are not independent, you are not free. When we are driven by ego, we do things that will project the right image and we become consumed with money, power, control, vanity—the worldly things that many people value. Your choices are not based on what is good but rather on what makes you look good. When you live to support an image, you are dependent on others to feed your ego. This is not freedom.

In Order to Feel Good, You Must *Do Good*: If You Set Out to Feel Good, You Often Wind Up Feeling Bad

Last, when you make a choice to do what is right, you feel good about yourself. This is because *to feel good you must do good,* not what feels good or looks good. Only when you are able to *choose responsibly* are you in charge of your life and do you gain self-respect. Then your actions are free and you feel good about who you are. Now we begin to bring to the surface the wonderful intricacies of self-esteem, ego, independence, and self-respect.

So we see that doing what is right nourishes our psyche. You gain self-respect and in return self-esteem. This is how self-respect and self-control are intertwined.

Here's How It All Fits Together

When someone does something to you that takes away some of your control or power, you get angry. If you have low self-esteem, then that means by definition that you do not feel in control. And you will be damned if someone is going to come along and rob you of your last few remaining drops of independence and power, of feeling in control. *If you just glanced at this paragraph, please reread it as it is at the foundation of all interpersonal conflicts.*

Any situation that you deem as directly disrespectful, or that robs you of your self-respect by taking away your power, forces you to react negatively. If you feel in control and hence have self-esteem, then you are *not* going to respond with anger. We see this because *the higher a person's self-esteem, the less angry he becomes in any given negative situation.*

When We Don't Respect Ourselves, We Can't Truly Love Ourselves, and So We Seek Love from Others to Fill the Void

This love that we need comes in the package of respect. If other people respect us, then we feel that we can respect ourselves as we "convert" their respect of us into *self-love*. Self-esteem and ego both pivot on *self-respect*. We need it from somewhere, and if we don't get it from ourselves we demand it from others.

Self-Esteem and Ego Are Inversely Related—When One Goes Up, the Other Goes Down

The part of us that seeks self-respect from others is called the *ego*. The ego is a projection of how we want and need the world to see us. With low self-esteem (meaning the ego is in charge), when we get "good" or positive feedback, we feel good about ourselves. When we don't, we feel less good about who we are.

When someone is rude or embarrasses us—does anything that is disrespectful—if we have low self-esteem, it causes us to question our own self-worth and lash out with anger. This is why a person with low self-esteem is highly sensitive—because his opinion of himself fluctuates with his ability to impress others.

Understand, it is only our ego—our false self—that gets offended. The greater our self-esteem, the less hurt we feel when someone is disrespectful.

When a person gets angry, it is because he is, to some extent, fearful. And this fear comes from the fact that he has lost control of some aspect of his life—of his circumstance, his understanding of his world, or his self-image. Anger is the impulsive response to this fear, which then sparks the conflict, feud, or disagreement because we direct our anger toward the source that we feel is responsible for robbing us of our power, our control.

WHY IS ANGER THE EMOTIONAL RESPONSE?

When we do not get respect from others, we get angry because it hurts how *we need to see ourselves*. It cuts off our "food" supply—our nourishment for the psyche. And this disrupts our ability to feel in control. The emotional response to this loss of control is fear. And the response to fear—the ego's attempt to compensate for the loss—is anger. At the root of all negative emotions—envy, lust, jealousy, and especially anger—is fear. At the root of fear is low self-esteem. *This is why angry people have low self-esteem.* This is why they argue, are stubborn, and don't forgive. *Anger makes us feel powerful.* It gives us the *illusion* that we are in control, free, and independent. But in reality it makes us lose control.

THE PARADOX OF RESPECT

In order to try to gain respect, people with low self-esteem do the very things that make other people lose respect for them. They brag about themselves and are arrogant. They are quick to judge, gossip, criticize, and embarrass others. But no one respects someone who puts people down and who's constantly seeking the approval of those around him. Not only do others think less of him, but he also winds up feeling worse about himself. Remember, this is because we gain self-respect by doing what we know to be right, and since deep down inside we know this gossiping and being judgmental is wrong, it moves us farther away from liking our self.

ANGER IS THE ILLUSION OF CONTROL

You know that when you become angry, you feel a sense of empowerment, but it is only a counterfeit of true confidence. We hold on to the anger because then we feel that we have control over the relationship. The person is now *dependent on us* to forgive. When we are hurt, we go into defense mode, and anger boosts the ego and gives us the sense of identity, control, and permanence that was taken away. It is an illusion that grounds us. It is our defense mechanism to feeling vulnerable. Yet in the end, it is still just an illusion and offers no real satisfaction or lasting psychological comfort.

HUMAN BEINGS HAVE A FUNDAMENTAL NEED FOR INDEPENDENCE: WHEN WE LOSE CONTROL, WE LOSE OUR SENSE OF INDEPENDENCE

Has there ever been a time in your life when you were dependent on others for most of your needs? This can usually make a person feel a little uncomfortable. It's hard to feel empowered and good about yourself when you're constantly on the receiving end.

Freedom is at the crux of self-respect. You can't feel good about yourself when you are constantly dependent on someone or something—from drugs to financial support. Think about how you feel when you have to go to someone for help—you can feel uneasy and anxious. Human beings need a *sense of independence* to feel good, and losing control robs us of our sense of empowerment. It pulls the rug out from under our psyche.

Therefore, to restore peace to any situation, you must *first restore that person's sense of independence.* (Don't worry, this is done in a matter of minutes.)

I WAS NAKED IN SCHOOL AGAIN
Two of the most common dreams people have are those of loose or missing teeth and being naked in a public place. What do these two themes share? *Fear of losing control*—being vulnerable and exposed. Consider, too, some common phobias: fear of flying, falling, snakes, and so on. Again, the common theme is feeling out of control.

This is why it is so hard for someone with low self-esteem to forgive. When a person is wronged, she goes into *protection mode,* where she is afraid to give of herself. And giving someone your trust, respect, and forgiveness is giving of your emotional self. Because some sense of her self-respect has been taken away, she feels less good about herself and more scared to *give*. Giving is a risk, and she is fearful of losing more of her self and her remaining self-respect. *So she holds back.* Hence another foundation of the psychological strategies we will use is to *build up* a person's psychological reserves so she can *give* again, freely and easily.

I'M TELLING YOU THE DICTIONARY IS WRONG!

Have you ever wondered why it is so important for someone to believe as he does despite obvious evidence to the contrary? He insists that the dictionary is wrong because it doesn't have the word he wants to put down in Scrabble. And playing Trivial Pursuit is a real treat when he has you half-convinced that there is a misprint on every other card. This person "needs" to be right for the same reason someone gets angry. He is unable to feel "less," to be wrong and to lose power. If you know this, it's much easier for you to detach from the situation, because you recognize that it's not about you or the game but that his ego needs to do this. This is about him, it's not about you. Have sympathy and compassion, and try not to get defensive, because then *your ego* is getting involved. See the situation for what it is.

CHAPTER 2

THE CONFLICT RECIPE

Let's now streamline what we've discussed and look at the underlying psychology behind how conflicts arise out of everyday situations and circumstances.

The conflict recipe contains four ingredients that ignite every single type of argument, conflict, feud, or estrangement. This sequence underscores the often unconscious motivation behind a person's response to any negative situation.

1. First there is the **event** or **catalyst.** In effect, the spark is that something is, or isn't, said or done; or something doesn't go the way we would like for it, or need for it, to go. Simply, a situation goes unexpectedly from how we desire or expected it to be.
2. This produces a **loss of control.**
3. Any person, in order to feel good about himself, needs a sense of independence. This loss of control robs a person of his sense of freedom and control, making him dependent and hence **fearful.**
4. This fear is the basis for our **anger.** Anger is only a response to fear; it is a psychological attempt to compensate for this loss of control. Oftentimes anger is also a mask for other emotions, such as jealousy, guilt, or shame.

THE DOCTOR WILL SEE YOU NOW

This holds true for physical pain as well as psychological. This is why we are more easily annoyed and frustrated when something hurts us. A migraine headache, for instance, is a pain that we are not in control of, and so a person may become readily angered and more easily provoked. And this is exactly why, while waiting in the doctor's office, we often "magically" *feel better,* because we know that relief is imminent. And this impending reinstatement of control is enough to put us at ease. The fact that your car stops making that funny noise when you bring it to the mechanic is an entirely different phenomenon well beyond the scope of this author's understanding.

REAL-WORLD, REAL-LIFE EXAMPLE AND SCENARIO

Let's look at a diverse set of circumstances that can produce a conflict and see how the psychological process unfolds in a consistently similar way.

- Your child runs into the street (catalyst) → you are not in control of what can happen → you get scared → and then become angry at your child.
- You trip over a chair in the dark (catalyst) → you lose control— meaning that your plan to walk from point A to point B without tripping was disrupted → this caused you to become scared, as you may have injured yourself → you then become angry. (Now what's interesting is that some people become angry at themselves, at the chair—kicking it—or at the person who put it there "for you to trip over." We'll see in just a bit what determines where and to whom or what you direct your anger.)
- Your spouse has an affair (catalyst). → This was not on your agenda (obviously), as it conflicts with how you expect a relationship to be, and you lose control of the relationship. → This causes you to become fearful of what happened to you, or might happen to you and to the relationship. → Consequently, you are angered.

- Someone cuts you off on the road (catalyst). → You lose control of the situation, as you had to swerve or hit your brakes in order to avoid an accident. → This causes you to become scared, thinking of "what could have happened." → The result is then anger at the other driver.
- Your child refuses to wear her warm jacket (catalyst). → You feel that you are not in control of the situation. → You may become fearful that she does not respect you and/or will not listen to other things that you ask her to do. → You then become angry with her for not listening to you.
- Someone tells you to shut up or curses at you (catalyst). → Depending on who it is, this act of disrespect may cause you to feel less good about yourself. → Depending on your own psyche, you become fearful that he doesn't like or respect you, and this causes you to question your own self-worth and image. → You become angered because how you wish for someone to treat and relate to you is different from how the situation is unfolding.

LADIES AND GENTLEMEN . . .

This is why public speaking is ranked as the number-one fear—even above death! Because the speaker is not in control of the audience's perception of her, she doesn't know what they are thinking about her, and this makes her fearful. For this reason, we can speak more easily one-on-one because we are able to see instantly the person's reaction and so we feel more in control of the situation. But as the size of the audience increases, the ability to accurately gauge the audiences' perception decreases. Feedback gives us direction and a greater sense of control.

CHAPTER 3

The Psychology at Play

The following is a complete review of the psychological mechanics behind any and all conflicts, feuds, and estrangements. These eighteen points outline the exact forces at work, crystallizing, summarizing, and *reinforcing* the intricate dynamics of the previous pages. (For a detailed examination of the psychology behind these, please go back to Chapters 1 and 2.)

1. All interpersonal conflicts have two major components: respect and control. Whether the issues involved concern lying, cheating, fairness, values, or beliefs, the core triggers are a lack of respect and the feeling that you are not in control of the situation.

2. The question, then, is why do we care? What is it about respect and control that are so fundamentally important to a person? The answer is . . .

3. We need to love ourselves in order to feel good about who we are. This love is called self-esteem.

4. Self-respect is the gateway to self-esteem. When we make good choices in life to do what is right over what is easy, over that which only makes us *look* good, we gain self-respect. And when we don't, we literally "like" ourselves less. *A person needs to respect himself* and his decisions in order to feel good about who he is.

5. When we don't make the right choice, it's because we are not in full and complete control of ourselves. We are either *giving in* to a body impulse or an ego drive. A body impulse can be

overeating or sleeping in excess. An ego drive can run the gambit from making a joke at someone's expense to working to buy a car that you cannot afford.

6. And what happens when we do this? We get angry at ourselves. When we're not in control of ourselves, we lose self-respect; our self-anger is just like our anger at others when they are disrespectful to us and/or when we lose control of the situation. And the more we crave respect and approval, the angrier we are apt to become. Now what does all this have to do with conflict, feuds, and estrangements?

7. The barometer that determines how annoyed, frustrated, or angered we become with others in any given situation is based on the degree to which we feel in control of ourselves and our lives. Our respect for ourselves, in short, determines (a) the amount of respect we crave from others and (b) our need to push for control and dominance.

8. We all give in to the urges of our body and our ego sometimes. But depending on how frequently and *recently* we did that, depending on the *overall proportion* of giving in to taking charge, that is the key to our response to outside conflict. When we "give in" to ourselves and in effect don't get what we *really* want, then we insist instead that the world be more accommodating. And so, specifically . . .

9. When *you* are in a situation that robs you of control, it causes you to react negatively because you feel insecure and you need to hold on to every drop of independence. And when you are in a situation where you feel disrespected, it causes a negative response because the outside world, through your ego, is your only source of psychological support or nourishment.

10. The more a person is in control of himself, the greater his self-respect and the higher his self-esteem. And vice versa. The more he gives in, the less good he feels about himself and the more intensely negative do his reactions become.

11. Since lack of self-respect is created by a lack of control, and human beings need a sense of control to effectively make choices, any situation that takes away control causes an angry reaction.

Additionally, any circumstances where you are disrespected, even without losing control, causes you to react negatively because then you need the respect of other people in order to feel good about yourself. As this respect is converted into a feeling of self-worth→self-respect→self-esteem→self-love, the more you like yourself, the less you care what others think of you. The lower your self-esteem, the more you need respect.

12. So we see that self-control is the gateway to self-respect. When a person is not in control, he loses respect for himself. And then it is up to the rest of the world to feed his psyche with the two components of respect and control so that he can feel good about who he is.

13. When we find ourselves in a situation that produces a loss of control or a lack of respect, we become fearful. This is because our psychological needs are not being met. This creates *fear.* The response to this fear is anger. And this anger sparks the conflict.

14. We all know this to be true in our own lives: When we feel good about how things are going, we are less easily angered. But when we're having a "bad" day, the slightest thing can set us off.

15. Now let's see how all of this psychology comes together to form specific techniques that can be used to resolve conflict. This is done far more quickly and easily because we're able to "feed" or gratify another person through a direct pipeline to their psyche that doesn't require years, months, weeks, or even days. Only minutes. How is this so?

16. The strategies in this book involve giving the other person the *ingredients* that his psyche needs to convert anger into self-love. These techniques create a situation where you not only restore this person's sense of well-being, but you also become the *source* of it. This *transforms* the way the person sees you and the situation and solidifies your ability to make peace.

17. We infuse the person with a sense of independence, control, respect, permanence—all things to bolster the psyche—in varying techniques and degrees, so that the psyche can use these as nourishment and convert them into respect and self-

love. And we've seen that the higher a person's self-esteem, the better equipped he is, and willing, to make peace. He doesn't need to hold on to anger and control, because he has the capacity to give. He is strong and independent enough to offer forgiveness, to give in, and to make peace.

18. Then, with his feeling of control and independence restored, fear disappears and his anger unravels. This allows the person to give up the need to control and allows him, if need be, to forgive actions against him. Once his emotions are assuaged, you can deal with the volatile issues quickly and rationally and resolve even the most hardened arguments, disagreements, conflicts, feuds, or estrangements.

STRESS BUSTERS

I'm sure it comes as no surprise to learn that under stress—emotional, financial, physical, or any sort—conflicts are more likely to occur. The reason is that stress comes from a build-up of feeling out of control. A person reaches his boiling point, so tolerance in general falls. Stress wears us out and makes us more prone to lash out. In times of high stress, it is good advice to be cautious of situations or conversations that might be better left for another time.

PART TWO

THE SOLUTION TO ALL
ARGUMENTS, CONFLICTS, FEUDS,
AND ESTRANGEMENTS . . . WITH
REAL-WORLD, REAL-LIFE EXAMPLES
AND SCENARIOS

SECTION I

KEEPING SPARKS FROM BECOMING FLAMES:
PUT OUT THE FIRE BEFORE IT EVEN BEGINS BY
HANDLING DIFFICULT PEOPLE, CONVERSATIONS,
AND SITUATIONS THE BEST WAY, RIGHT AWAY

Whether you want to keep a difference of opinion from escalating into an argument, or give criticism without causing hurt feelings, learn the psychological secrets to deal with any difficult person, situation, or conversation—easily, calmly, and quickly. These are situations and conversations that can spark an argument. So it makes sense to extinguish the possibility before it ever arises, as it's easier to avoid a conflict than to end one.

There are two ways to put an airplane on the ground. You can either land it or crash it—either way, it's on the ground. It is the approach, however, that is everything. You can avoid many serious feuds and disagreements by shifting how you approach the person, conversation, or situation that might produce a conflict.

Handle these situations right from the beginning and you will shut down a problem before it even begins.

Remember, relationships are built on trust, honesty, and respect, so make sure your motivations are good and the benefits to all parties are clear. Please see "A Note to Readers" (page xv) for further clarification of this necessity.

CHAPTER 4

RESOLVE ANY PERSONALITY CONFLICT IN MINUTES

Your objective may or may not be to save this person from himself. For whatever reason—whether you have to work with him or you want to keep peace in the family—you want to avoid a conflict. Either way you can use this strategy to avoid a problem before it even begins.

Here's a general rule of thumb: If a person dislikes you without good reason, it's not because she doesn't like you, but because she doesn't like herself very much. The arrogant, loud, obnoxious, and rude person who has no respect for other people—or you specifically—really has no respect for herself. Therefore you can turn a lion into a lamb by changing how she feels about *herself*, which then changes how she feels about you. And it's as easy as 1-2-3.

When a person doesn't like herself much, there is no self-love or self-esteem. And as we've discussed in the previous chapter, this causes her to filter her world through this distorted lens. Whenever someone acts rudely or cruelly to you, it's always because of one or a combination of three major motivations, all involving—to no one's surprise—the ego, and it manifests from a diminished sense of self-worth.

- *He thinks you dislike him.* You may have unintentionally not given him your full attention, or he misinterpreted a look or something you said or did. It doesn't take much for a person with low self-esteem to determine that you don't like him. As he doesn't like himself very much, he assumes—at an unconscious level, of course—that other people must feel the same way.
- *He feels threatened by you.* A fragile ego is envious and jealous, and

you may remind him of what he wants but doesn't have. To reconcile these feelings of inadequacy he "implants" you with negative traits and consequently dislikes you for them. For instance, if Joe is envious of Melvin because he is rich, handsome, and successful, then Joe will "see" something in Melvin, maybe arrogance or impatience, amplify it, and then dislike Melvin for being this way.

- *He sees in you traits in himself that he dislikes.* Hence—albeit unconsciously—he dislikes you as you remind him of what he doesn't like about himself.

SOME ADDITIONS TO THE RULE

There are three other motivations that are possible. Even though the themes are varied, in the psychology behind them they are consistent with one another and with the above. Therefore the techniques used in this section work for these motivations as well and are mentioned to provide a comprehensive look at the possible motivations for a personality conflict. (1) Your basic garden variety prejudice can, of course, cause a person to dislike you. (2) If he wants to help you and is unable to, this feeling of helplessness can turn to guilt. The person then grows to dislike you, for his frustration with his inability to help causes him to take it out on you, the source. (3) When we are interested in someone romantically, sometimes we don't know what to do with our feelings and may act cruelly so that the person won't think we like her. Because if she did, then we would lose leverage and be at a psychological disadvantage. I know it seems like high school all over again, but people are people, and some don't grow up.

STRATEGIC PSYCHOLOGICAL SOLUTION

It is very, very hard to dislike someone who not only likes us but *respects* us as well. Have you ever had the experience of having someone whom you don't particularly like pay you a huge compliment? Or he asks for your advice—presumably out of respect for your opinion?

Suddenly you find yourself forced to reevaluate your feelings toward him and adjust them to be more favorable. Because if he's a fool and he asks us for advice, then that would mean that someone who doesn't know what he is doing is coming to us for advice. We'd rather adjust our thinking of *him* and conclude that maybe he's not such a bad guy after all.

This is known as *reciprocal affection*. We tend to admire, respect, and like someone once we are told that they have these same feelings for us.

PHASE 1: ESTABLISH MUTUAL RESPECT

To adjust anyone's thinking about you, tell a third party, maybe a mutual friend, what it is that you honestly *like* and *respect* about this person or how you admire her for something she's done or even stands for. Once this information makes its way to her, you will simply be amazed at how fast she becomes an ally. Whether it's a coworker, boss, assistant, neighbor, sibling, child, mechanic—*everyone needs to feel appreciated.* Let this third party know your genuine warm feelings toward her and watch the magic happen.

You may be thinking, Why can't I just go and tell her myself? Why all this cloak-and-dagger stuff with a third party? The reason is that you run the risk of her thinking that you're insincere or "trying to get her to like you." When we hear something from a third party, we rarely question the veracity of what we're told.

I LOVE SQUARE DANCING, TOO!

It is not true that opposites attract. We actually are more inclined to like people who are similar to us and who have similar interests, beliefs, and values. We may find someone interesting who is different from us, but it's what you share that produces a psychological bond. When you speak to this person, talk about what you both enjoy and what you have in common. Note: Try to find positive commonalties. Negative interests, though mutual, may create an unpleasant association with you.

PHASE 2: ALLOW THE PERSON TO GIVE TO YOU

Next, follow up your kind words by expressing an interest in this person's *helping you* with something. We often think that people will like us if we do nice things for them, but the reality is that a person actually likes you more after he does something for you. This is for several reasons: (1) Whenever we invest ourselves in anything, in this case a person—with time, energy, attention—we feel closer and more attached. (2) When someone allows us to give, we feel better about ourselves, as giving reinforces the feeling that we are in control and independent. (3) And finally, doing for another engages a psychological phenomenon called cognitive dissonance, whereby we conclude—partly unconsciously—that we must have a favorable impression of him. Otherwise, we're going around doing things for people we don't like. We'd rather conclude that the person is worthy of our investment.

PHASE 3: SHOW YOUR HUMAN SIDE

Studies show something fascinating when it comes to human conflicts. Often, in an attempt to get someone to like us, we'll engage in what is called self-enhancement behavior. This is when we tell and show the other person how wonderful we are, so that he will come to like us. Yet when you're dealing with a person who feels threatened, research clearly indicates, *self-deprecating* behavior is the optimum attitude. This would be offering information about yourself that *isn't* flattering. It shows humility, honesty, and trust—three things that promote a successful resolution to any personality conflict.

REAL-WORLD, REAL-LIFE EXAMPLE AND SCENARIO

To a *mutual party,* relay what you genuinely like and respect about the person with whom you are having difficulty. Follow this with a request for his help. This will also allow you to find out if the message was effectively relayed, as he will then seek you out to help you with what you need.

A. *"I'm so impressed with the way Jim dealt with the advertisers in the meeting. Do you think he'd give me some sales tips?"*
B. *"I'm so proud of Suzy for sticking to her guns on that issue. I'd love to talk to her about how I can be more assertive."*
C. *"Dr. Witherspoon is really someone I can count on for getting things done. Do you think he'd talk to some of the other doctors about time management?"*
D. *"The way she keeps her home, it should be in* House & Garden. *Do you think she'd give me some decorating tips?"*

Then . . . when in the conversation with the person with whom you are having difficulties, listen intently, ask questions, and talk about what you might have in common. Additionally, at an appropriate time, share something true and mildly embarrassing, such as:

> *"I ran into my neighbor and completely blanked on his name when I introduced him to my friend."* Or *"I was so embarrassed, I walked right out of the record store with a CD in my pocket."*

※ **FLASH REVIEW** ※

If someone dislikes you without an apparent reason, it's because they feel that *you* dislike them or they in some way feel threatened by you, or you remind them of traits they don't like in themselves. The solution is to make the person *feel good* about himself— through praise, having him invest in you, and self-deprecating behavior. This evokes a powerful psychological principle whereby he alters his feelings toward you—to more favorable ones—in an unconscious attempt to reconcile that he feels good about himself *because of you.* Therefore, you must be a good person.

CHAPTER 5

How to Ignore Someone's Advice Without Causing Hurt Feelings

Have you ever wondered why some people get so infuriated when you don't take their advice? Advice by definition is something that is *offered*. It is merely a suggestion. And yet sometimes if you don't respond "just right," a person can become extremely offended. This is especially true with someone who is overly sensitive, to the point that nothing you can say other than "That's the best idea I've ever heard" will suffice.

This is because he feels that it is not the *advice* that you are dismissing or rejecting, but *him*. Therefore, even if the input sounds incredibly ludicrous, use this strategy and keep good relations.

STRATEGIC PSYCHOLOGICAL SOLUTION

PHASE 1: SHOW APPRECIATION FOR THE INPUT

Thank the person for her suggestion and tell her that you will think about it. Even if you disagree with the advice and think it's a bad idea, allow her the dignity of feeling that you are going to consider it. (You may even be surprised that she is in fact right after all.)

PHASE 2: GIVE TWO REASONS WHY YOU AGREE AND ONE REASON WHY YOU DON'T

A day or so later, offer her *two* reasons why she is right and then *one* reason why her idea doesn't make sense. Remember, she is not on commission, so she offers advice for your benefit—it makes her feel good to contribute—and only becomes upset if she feels that you don't have enough faith or trust in her judgment. This phase eliminates *completely* her feeling that you are rejecting her.

PHASE 3: THANK HER FOR GETTING YOU THINKING

Tell her that you've decided already to make *another change,* and her initial suggestion is what got you thinking, sparking this new idea. Now she feels part of the decision-making process and is not offended that her specific idea was not taken.

PHASE 4: SEEK OUT HER OPINION ON SOMETHING ELSE

To solidify the strategy, follow up by asking for her opinion on something else—related or unrelated to this situation. If at all possible, choose something that you could easily do or not do, depending on her answer. This concretizes in her mind that you respect her and that it was just one idea that you did not particularly agree with.

REAL-WORLD, REAL-LIFE EXAMPLE AND SCENARIO

SCENARIO: A secretary suggests to her boss that it might be a good idea to redecorate the waiting area. She's says to her boss, "Jim, I think our clients would have a better image of us if we redid the lobby and made it more modern." Jim likes the Old World look and charm and has no desire to change it.

> **JIM:** *"That's an interesting idea, Sally. Let me give that some thought."* In most cases, Sally, inspired by Jim's consideration, will continue to try to "sell him" on the idea.

> [The next day] **JIM:** *"Sally, I thought about what you said, and a more modern look might attract some people, and it would be nice to*

look at something different, but I think this motif projects a good image for us."

[After a brief pause] *"But your suggestion got me thinking that we should make some changes around here and replace that sign on the door for one that's a little classier. Thanks a lot for your suggestion about how to improve things around here. Without it, the sign idea never would have occurred to me. Keep thinking! Oh, and also I wanted to get your opinion on something else. What do you think about giving the place a new paint job?"*

He considered her input, and showed that he valued her and her idea. Think about how different her reaction would have been had he merely dismissed her suggestion out of hand. For those times when you're dealing with sensitive people, this technique will prove invaluable—especially when it saves you from resentment and greater aggravation.

NOT IN A THOUSAND YEARS!

If a suggestion is made that you don't even want to consider, and you don't want to give the impression that it's even remotely possible, then say the following: "You know you're the third person to tell me that in the past few weeks. I hear what you're saying, but I just don't see it." By letting her know that *other people* have suggested the same thing, it dramatically dilutes the rejection of her idea, as it is not technically "her" idea—others have said the same thing and you dismissed it from them as well.

※ FLASH REVIEW ※

You can disregard someone's advice as long as the person does not feel as if you are ignoring or rejecting *him*. A person is offended because he feels it is not the advice that you are dismissing but him. Therefore, simply offer two reasons why you agree with him and one why you would prefer to do it your way. Then thank her for getting you thinking about the "situation" in general and how it led you to another great idea. Follow this up with a solicitation of his opinion on something else, so that he knows you do respect him and just aren't going with this one idea.

CHAPTER 6

In Business, Turn Any Complaint into a Plus

Rolling your eyes, tapping your foot, and crossing your arms may offer a degree of satisfaction, but you'll pay for it later. When a person complains about something trivial, what she is really saying is "I'm too important to be treated like this." If her unconscious thinking is *Maybe I deserve this* and it causes her to question her own self-worth, she will become *very irritated*. As we know, when this "treatment" is personalized, a person can begin to feel invalidated and is easily agitated.

Of course, the person may have a legitimate gripe, and any person would feel unjustly injured. In any case, you can use this strategy to smooth over even the most ruffled of feathers.

STRATEGIC PSYCHOLOGICAL SOLUTION

You want to address the person's ego more than the actual problem. Especially if the "problem" is something inconsequential or blown out of proportion.

PHASE 1: SIMPLY LISTEN

Listen. Don't agree, disagree, or argue. Even if he's partly to blame, hold off on saying that anything is his fault. If you say anything other than "I'm sorry" while he's still upset, he'll get more defensive and argumentative. It's like explaining to someone how he should eat healthfully and exercise regularly while he is having a heart attack. First solve the problem at hand and then address the issues that got you there. *Do not get defensive, or you will get an argument.* Sometimes he just needs to get it off his chest, so let him speak. Other times he's looking for a fight. If you don't interrupt, he will run out of things to say.

PHASE 2: PARAPHRASE AND EMPATHIZE

Paraphrase back what you've just been told to crystallize his complaint and to show that you have been listening and you understand. You want to empathize with him. Do not say, "This never happened before" and that you are so surprised. Why? Because then he's thinking, *Why am I the only poor slob this has happened to?*

PHASE 3: ASK *HIM* FOR A FAVOR

That's right. Ask him to do something for you that shows you take what he said seriously. This does an interesting thing: It conveys the message that you are *making his problem your problem.* We'll give an example soon to clarify this phase.

PHASE 4: DO SOMETHING SPECIAL

This is a great way to calm him down. Let him know that you are going to do something special for him to make up for this "travesty." But don't tell him exactly what it is—let it be a surprise. You will notice that he calms down quickly for several reasons. First, everyone likes surprises. He's gone from mad to a little excited. Second, he can't argue with you that it's not enough, because he doesn't even know what it is. And third, if it's something really great, he doesn't want to risk losing it by being too angry with you. Once he's calmed down, you can better gauge the situation and decide on the appropriate compensation.

REAL-WORLD, REAL-LIFE EXAMPLE AND SCENARIO

SCENARIO: As a hotel manager, you are confronted by a guest who was not told until the next day that his urgent fax had arrived at the front desk.

First, you of course listen intently without interrupting. And then you paraphrase back what he's told you.

> *"So, Mr. Smith, we had your fax sitting at the desk the entire time? I am terribly sorry. I'm so embarrassed that this happened to you. You have my complete assurance that I will be personally responsible for your comfort and needs during the rest of your stay. And I was wondering, sir, if you might do me a favor. The vice president of hotel operations would want to know what happened directly from you. Do you think I could ask you to tell him yourself exactly what happened?"*

> [Toward the end of the discussion]. *"And I've thought of the perfect way to apologize appropriately. It's a surprise and I don't want to spoil it, but I think you will enjoy it immensely."*

Look what happened here. Mr. Smith was irate that nobody cared enough to tell him about his fax, and now *he's so important* that the vice president of the hotel wants to speak with him. It shows that they are taking him *seriously,* and that is what he wants. He's now probably thinking, *Wow, they sure are making a big deal about this little fax problem.*

✳ FLASH REVIEW ✳

When a person complains about something trivial, it is because his sense of self and independence has been damaged. He wants to be heard. His ego demands that he is given respect and that he is validated. *So give it to him.* In every case, assuaging the ego will calm him down and in many cases eliminate the entire problem. Unfounded complaints or criticism have little to do with the circumstance or situation, and much to do with the person—particularly his ego.

CHAPTER 7

WHEN ASKED FOR YOUR OPINION: WHAT TO SAY WHEN THERE'S NOTHING NICE TO SAY

We've all been there. Someone asks us our advice and we know that if we say what we're *really* thinking we're heading for a scene. The fact is that if a person comes to you and asks you what you think of his new custom-made suit, he's not asking you for your opinion—he's asking for a compliment, or a confirmation of the fact that he has made the right choice. If he wanted your opinion, he would have brought you swatches of fabric so you could help him decide.

STRATEGIC PSYCHOLOGICAL SOLUTION

So here's what you do. If someone asks for your opinion about something after the fact—meaning there is nothing that can be done—*give him a compliment*. It's what he's really asking for anyway. However, if he's asking for your input so he can *avoid* making a mistake or so he can do what is right, then you have an obligation to be honest. Honesty without the commonsense judgment of whether you are being asked for a compliment or for input is senseless.

In situations where you're sparing someone's feelings or avoiding embarrassment, it's perfectly sensible not to be completely honest. If you are truthful, and you have a negative opinion, and the person can't do anything about the situation, you will just cause resentment and hurt feelings. Don't think you're being virtuous by being honest in situations where the person cannot take advantage of your advice.

REAL-WORLD, REAL-LIFE EXAMPLE AND SCENARIO

QUESTIONS WHERE A COMPLIMENT OR PRAISE IS IN ORDER

Q "What do you think of my daughter's piano playing?"
A "It's just lovely."

Q "How do you like my new patio furniture?"
A "It's beautiful."

Q "Isn't my wife a great cook?"
A "One of the best."

QUESTIONS WHERE THE TRUTH IS IN ORDER

Q "We're thinking of naming our baby girl Sparky. What do you think?"
A "I don't think that's a great choice."

Q Do you think this charity does good work? I was thinking of donating money to them."
A "I've heard mixed things. You may want to check further."

Q "I'm looking at a 1980 Ford Pinto for $26,000. Is that a good deal?"
A "It doesn't sound like you're getting a great price. I would pass on it."

Although the above scenarios are silly common sense, it is good to remind ourselves that honesty is not always the best policy. Doing what is right, however, is.

* FLASH REVIEW *

If your advice will help to save the person from any type of harm—physical, emotional, financial, etc.—then you have an obligation to be truthful. However, if it's after the fact, and nothing can be done, then honesty is not the best policy. Offer a compliment or kind word instead, because that is what the person is really looking for.

CHAPTER 8

Handle Annoying Nonsense Criticism
Smoothly and Simply

Ahhh, there's nothing like it: Comments from the proverbial peanut gallery. What do you do when someone is simply busting your chops, giving you nonsense criticism, or commenting on something ridiculous? And she's doing it in such a condescending and patronizing way that you want to dismiss it, but you want to do it politely and without sounding more obnoxious than she does. For instance, your mother-in-law says, "You know, darling, my boy likes to eat real food. Maybe a cooking class would do you some good?" Maybe she's saying it to get a rise out of you, or maybe she's partly sincere. What to do?

STRATEGIC PSYCHOLOGICAL SOLUTION

The solution is very simple. You thank the person for offering her insight, and then later you decide whether or not there is any credence to what she said. Sometimes it can be hard to separate out the message from the messenger, but when you do, you may find some good advice.

Our first instinct is to get defensive and argue with the person. But the bottom line is who cares. Thank the person regardless of how insane or self-serving the remark is. If you get defensive, then you have an argument. And recognize that if the advice is more of a put-down than it is constructive, she is coming from a place of pain and needs to do this in order to feel good about herself. Have compassion and empathy for her and rise above it. There's no reason to argue. You really have to see this person as an emotionally challenged six-year-old and speak to her as if she were. If she needs to say this to feel good, then she is hurting. The pain seeps out into comments like these. If you get angry or annoyed, it's the same as kicking the shins of a ninety-year-old man who wants to pick a fight with you. First, no matter what happens, you can't win. And second, *what are you doing?* Do not get defensive. Do not engage her. Simply:

1. Say thank you sincerely and directly.
2. Ask a question regarding *how* or *why* she herself is so capable, without being sarcastic!

The person who insists on verbally denigrating you needs to be treated as someone who is not emotionally well. And best of all, in a short time this strategy will put an end to most of her future comments.

REAL-WORLD, REAL-LIFE EXAMPLE AND SCENARIO

COMMENT: *"You know, Rich, you were way off your game in that meeting."*
RESPONSE: *"Really? I'll have to review that later. You're so great for looking out for me. How would you have handled it?"*

COMMENT: *"Denise, you know that outfit is not very flattering on you."*
RESPONSE: *"Oh, thanks for letting me know. A lot of friends wouldn't tell me something like that because they'd think I might get upset. You're such a special person. Where did you get such a great sense of fashion from?"*

COMMENT: *"I thought you were trying to lose weight. Do you think you should be eating that?"*
RESPONSE: *"Oh, you're so sweet for remembering that I'm dieting. Thank you. You seem like you have great willpower. I'd love for you to tell me your secret."*

You see, this person, while being disrespectful to you, does so because she craves respect herself. She needs to be heard and to feel good about herself. By making a nonsense negative comment to you, she accomplishes this. Knocking someone down is the fastest way to feel better about ourselves—but it's an illusion. And you, by thanking him and asking him for his input, feed his psyche and end the "attack."

Of course, you want to remember that all criticism does not come from people in pain. And just because it's not done in a caring way does not mean that this person doesn't still care about you. She may not be psychologically balanced and so isn't able to critique you effectively and kindly, even though she cares—and therefore it sounds as if it's an unkind and unfair attack.

✳ FLASH REVIEW ✳

The best way to deal with nonsensical criticism is to derail the conversation and feed the person's ego. To do this, you simply thank the person and ask her advice on what she thinks is the best way for you to achieve an optimum outcome.

CHAPTER 9

The Psychological Secret to Criticizing *Anyone* About Anything, Without Ever Offending

There are two ways to give criticism—a right way and a wrong way—and how you do it can make all the difference in the world. As you may have experienced in your own life, sometimes you are open to criticism and other times the slightest critique will make you feel like crawling under a rock or make you extremely defensive and argumentative.

The ego is at the crux, because it is the only part of us that gets injured. The truth does not need protection from the outside world. Only this ego or shell, the projection of how we would like to appear, is subject to harm. Therefore if you bypass the ego—meaning that you don't make his problem about him but about *you*—you never have to worry about hurting his feelings.

STRATEGIC PSYCHOLOGICAL SOLUTION

This is one of the most amazing and effective techniques to radically change a person's perception of a situation. With this tactic the person will *positively* not be offended and not take your criticism personally whatsoever. And many times he may wind up feeling *better* about himself and the situation. The best way to give criticism is to *not* criticize. Instead, you *give praise*! And *still* accomplish your objective.

PHASE 1: LAY THE GROUNDWORK

The technique works like this. You first tell the person that you *really like* and/or *enjoy* or *appreciate* the way he is or what he does (whatever it is that you want him to change). Whether it's the seasoning of the food, his sexual position, or the way he prepares his reports. Whatever it is, tell him that you fully think it's *great.*

PHASE 2: JUMP SHIP

Then, after some time passes, tell the person that *you* changed *your mind* and would like him to do it, or try it, differently. Your motivation can be new information—for example, you recently read an article— or just being in the mood to try something new. In this way the onus is on you. It is no longer about him doing something wrong, so he can't be offended. Rather, it's about *you* changing *your* mind. It completely removes him—and hence his ego—from the equation. You see, by making it about you and not him, you make it nearly impossible for him to be offended.

> ### REAL-WORLD, REAL-LIFE EXAMPLE AND SCENARIO

SCENARIO A: A wife doesn't like the way her husband makes her breakfast. The omelet is always too spicy. But she feels that if she tells him, it will hurt his feelings.

> **WIFE:** *"Honey, I really love your omelets. You make them just perfect."*
>
> **HUSBAND:** *"Thank you!"* [Some time passes—a day or so]
>
> **WIFE:** [before he prepares breakfast] *"You know what, I was reading somewhere that spices can contribute to certain kinds of arthritis, and mine has been acting up lately. If you're up to the challenge, let's see if you can make it as tasty as always without the usual spices. I know it won't taste the same, but if it helps my arthritis, it*

would be worth the sacrifice." [Afterward] *"Wow, I didn't think it could get any better, but it's more delicious,* and *without the spices."*

You see, had she initially suggested that he change what he was doing, he might have been offended. But because she first reassured him that he was doing good, the change of approach has to do with *her* and *not him,* so it's almost impossible for him to be offended.

SCENARIO B: An executive thinks his longtime receptionist is a bit too abrupt with his clients, and he would like her to be a bit warmer and friendlier. Knowing how sensitive she is, he feels he cannot be direct in his criticism.

> **MR. JONES:** *You know, Ginger, I've been meaning to tell you that I received a nice compliment for you, about how efficient you are with the clients."*
> **GINGER:** *"Thank you, Mr. Jones."*

> **MR. JONES:** [later in the day] *"Oh, by the way, I'm expecting some folks from VEX, Inc. to be coming by. They're a real laid-back company, so do me a favor and chat with them a little bit to make them feel extra welcome."*
> **GINGER:** *Of course."*

> **MR. JONES:** [later that day, after the new client has left] *"Ginger, I hope I don't drive you nuts, but the folks from VEX, Inc. really enjoyed speaking with you and felt really comfortable. Being that you're so personable, let's try more of this chitchat stuff with the other clients and see how it goes."*

NEED AN OPENING?

What about those times when you want to bring up a subject but it's a little touchy in that your criticism is not necessarily a matter of preference or taste, but rather something that would be offensive to anyone? If you want to talk to someone about anything from his lack of patience with the kids to bad breath, do this: Ask him for advice on the very subject *for yourself* if practical, and if not, for a friend or relative.

You would say something such as, "Mike, I'd like your advice on something personal. Do you know how I can *X*? Or do a better job of *Y*? Or eliminate *Z*? This gives you an opening for the discussion, and he will invariably turn to himself as an example, since *he's the one giving you the advice.* When he does, you can talk to him about it. Let's say that you have a friend who is a nonstop gossip. To follow through, you would say something such as, "Do you think I gossip too much? I've been trying to work on cutting down a bit. Any suggestions for me?" If you approach the situation in this way, the conversation doesn't make him defensive, because he's not defending himself, he's only helping you. However, you are now able to talk to him about *why he does what he does.*

✴ FLASH REVIEW ✴

To avoid offending a person with even the harshest of criticism, simply make it about you and not her. To do this, first tell her that you love the way she does "it," and you then change *your mind* and tell her that you would like for her to try it a different way. She can only take it personally if it's about her—which it's not. When you put the onus on you, she cannot feel hurt or offended.

CHAPTER 10

Passive Aggression: The Thirty-Second Technique to Deal with People Who Won't Deal

What exactly is passive-aggressive behavior? As it relates here, it describes a person who does not choose to confront situations or conflicts directly and head-on. Rather, she "gets back at the person" indirectly by causing harm or inconvenience in a seemingly innocent manner. For instance, if Terri feels that her husband doesn't give her the respect she wants, even though she is bothered, she feels unable to speak with him directly about it. Therefore, she, partly unconsciously, may dress poorly or burn his dinner as a way of settling the score.

In general there are four ways a person can choose to respond to a disagreement: (1) retreat, (2) accept, (3) surrender, or (4) fight.

A passive-aggressive person is generally described as one who would *retreat* to avoid the confrontation. She is unable to confront the person and the situation head-on, so she chooses to back down, only to "get back at the person" in another way, at another time, whether it is by being late, "forgetting" to do something important for the person, or just generally inconveniencing her.

The second possible response is *accept*. She understands the full reality of the situation and those involved and responds responsibly and productively. And though she acts appropriately and fairly, given the situation, she does not become angered and emotional. This is the healthiest response, because she sees the situation as it is and does not allow her ego to take control.

A third possible response is *surrender*. This is where she simply gives up and gives in. This response often produces codependency and a doormat mentality in the relationship. She doesn't feel worthy to stand up for herself and/or feels that she is unable to advance her own agenda, needs, and wishes.

And last, the fourth is *fight*. Here we have the response that produces direct conflict. This person chooses to battle it out, emotionally charged and enraged.

STRATEGIC PSYCHOLOGICAL SOLUTION

There are two methods for handling passive-aggressive behavior. For times when you're dealing with someone where you don't want to "get to the bottom" of his issues or it's just someone who you don't feel is open to help, then go with Option A. With this approach your tactic is purely psychological and you eliminate the problem without creating a larger one.

This is done by letting the person know that you believe her motivations are grounded in something much more pathetic then merely wanting to unconsciously annoy you. And because she suffers from a lowered self-image (which is why she's doing what she's doing in the first place), she will always go with the lesser of two evils.

REAL-WORLD, REAL-LIFE EXAMPLE AND SCENARIO

SCENARIO: Sarah's coworker Jane constantly misplaces the files.

> **SARAH:** *"I want you to know, Jane, that I care about you as a friend, and this is why I want to talk with you about something. I hope this isn't embarrassing for you, but it may make you feel good to talk about it."*
>
> **JANE:** *"What on earth are you talking about?"*
>
> **SARAH:** *"I think I've realized what has going been on here. Why you keep misplacing the files."* [Take your pick]:
>   *"You're dyslexic."*
>   *"You don't know the alphabet."*

> *"There's so much stress at work that you can't concentrate."*
> *"You're having problems at home."*
> **JANE:** *"You're out of your mind. Everyone makes mistakes."*

> **SARAH:** *Okay, I'm sorry. I see I've upset you. Let's just forget about it. I hope things work out okay."*
> **JANE:** [wearing a fake smile] *"You didn't upset me. It's fine."*

Now look what Sarah accomplished. She made Jane aware that constant blundering has been noticed. The only way Jane can avoid Sarah thinking that she is right—which her ego won't like her to do—is to stop making the mistakes she was making. In this way, she can prove to Sarah that "everything is just fine with her." You see, the only way Jane can prove that she is right, and that there's nothing wrong, is by now filing correctly. (Please see Chapter 1 for an alternate approach.)

OPTION B: BUT WHAT IF *I DO* CARE?

If you want to know what is happening on a deeper level, and you feel that it would benefit the relationship if you were able to move past this issue, then go with Option B. Here you confront the person head-on. Since she is passive-aggressive and by definition runs from confrontation, you will find a short conversation may ensue. The key, though, is to give her what she doesn't feel she has: vast appreciation and respect for who she is. (See Chapters 11 and 12 for ways to effectively communicate this.) Additionally, give her the opportunity to know that she can talk to you about anything that might be bothering her. This one-two punch will pave the way for a longer, sincere, and meaningful conversation in the near future.

✳ FLASH REVIEW ✳

Dealing with people who refuse to deal does not have to be a lifelong challenge. The simple technique of offering an alternative motivation that is far worse than her unconscious intent forces the person—albeit mostly unconsciously—to stop the behavior, as it is the only way for her to prove that she is right and you are wrong.

CHAPTER 11

THE SECRET TO HANDLING THE ANGRY PERSON WHO IS (AMAZINGLY) NEVER WRONG

When something goes wrong, it's never him and it's always you. Sound familiar? When he gets like this, and you have to walk on eggshells and avoid looking at him the wrong way, use this surefire strategy to avoid an argument and eliminate these situations from happening again.

All of these encounters can be potentially explosive, but they can also be quickly extinguished just by saying the right thing. The reason why he becomes annoyed has almost nothing to do with the misunderstanding but rather a conclusion that he draws, whether or not the *intent* behind the person's action was accidental or purposeful.

The same situation can unfold a hundred times, and if it involves someone who can do no wrong, then the matter is dropped quickly. If it is with someone who can do no right, then you're heading down the path of an argument. Therefore, you simply want to be put into the category of one who can do no wrong. How do you do this? It's easier than you think, and it can be done *after the fact*. Anytime you know that you're not to blame, or no one is—in other words, it's just one of those things—then simply and quickly have him see you in the "right light."

A person who can do no wrong is one who we feel respects us. Obviously, any misunderstanding would have to be unintentional, because why would it have occurred?

Ahhh, but someone who doesn't treat us right? His motivation, even when he does right, is somehow always suspect.

The core of this person's behavior lies with low self-esteem. He feels that anything that happens must somehow relate to someone taking advantage of him. For instance, if you keep him waiting, he is likely to assume that you don't care enough or respect him enough to be on time.

When you have higher self-esteem, you are not as quick to ascribe the motivations as being personal but rather are more likely to believe that there was a problem on the other person's end. Or you understand that maybe he has his own hang-ups and needs to keep people waiting in an unconscious attempt to feel important. Simply, (a) you don't assume that his actions mean he doesn't respect you, and (b) should you come to that conclusion, you aren't angered, because you don't *need* his respect in order to respect yourself.

I *HAVE* TO SEE WHAT HE LOOKS LIKE

By the way, *this* is why, when someone cuts us off on the road, we want to see what he looks like. The action itself is often open to interpretation, but if he "looks" like someone who did this on purpose because he doesn't respect us, we get angrier. We assume his intentions as purposeful and not accidental. If a little old lady is the driver, we're not very angry, because we assume that she just didn't see us and so we don't take it so personally. Additionally, we want to see the person to confirm our stereotype of *who* would drive this way, as this boosts our feeling of control—the ability to "know" things and to be right.

With low self-esteem, the thinking, albeit often at an unconscious level is, *The person didn't care enough or like me enough or respect me enough to do what was right.* The more accepting we are of ourselves, the more accepting we are of others. Our world is filtered through our image of ourselves, and when that image is distorted, our relationships become distorted as well.

Low self-esteem causes a person to become self-absorbed, because she feels the whole world revolves around her and she thinks only in terms of her wants and needs.

Remember, in the beginning of the book, we said that self-respect is the foundation of self-esteem. Simply, if you do not respect yourself, you cannot respect anyone else. This is because we *give* respect to others. If you do not respect yourself, then what do you have to give? And with a lack of perceived mutual respect, you assume that the action was *intentional*.

STRATEGIC PSYCHOLOGICAL SOLUTION

If you're tired of "You made me miss the turn." Or "Why did you order me that? You know I can't eat fried food." Or "Why weren't the files finished? You had all night to get it done." Then read on . . .

The solution is simple. But before we get to that, we should say that no one has the right to abuse you. If you feel that you are someone's psychological punching bag, then change things. And know that people will treat you the way you train them to. If you're dealing with anyone remotely reasonable, let him know that his behavior is unacceptable.

That said, let's focus on the dynamics where you may not have the leverage to do that—such as dealing with your boss, your spouse, or a delicate family relationship, such as with an in-law.

The solution is to give this person what he craves at times when he's *not* upset. Then, when a situation becomes contentious, you will have built up his psychological reserve so that he won't find it necessary to lash out. He may choose another target, but not you. The reason is because, with this strategy, you become his source of psychological nourishment. Therefore, he is unable to bite the proverbial hand that feeds his psyche.

PHASE 1: BUILD UP RESPECT

The best defense is a strong offense. Build up his psychological reserves so that he can draw on them when he needs to. Here are some simple ways to do this. In your interactions and conversations:

- Criticize only when necessary, using the techniques discussed in Chapter 9.
- When he makes a mistake, be supportive and not hypercritical.

- Be considerate and polite in conversations.
- Don't gossip about him to anyone.
- Let other people know your genuine respect and admiration for him.
- Never belittle him, roll your eyes, or do anything disrespectful, especially around others.

While these are simple in content they can be difficult in execution. But their role in transforming your relationship can be dramatic.

PHASE 2: RESHAPE HIS SELF-CONCEPT

We'll talk more about the psychology of this in Chapter 14, so let's just review what to do specifically here. You want to get him to see himself in a way that is *consistent* with someone who does not lash out and blame you for his problems.

This is done with a simple, well-orchestrated phrase. In this case we want the person to see himself as someone who is easygoing, so you would say something like, "I so admire how cool you are when things get crazy around here." Or "I want you to know that I truly appreciate your patience with me."

This invokes the powerful psychological law of internal consistency. These phrases, and ones like it, make the person *feel compelled to follow through* on your image of him, because you involve the ego and create a sense of desired consistency. People have an inherent need to perform in a manner consistent with how they see themselves and with how they think others perceive them. I know it seems so simple, but the studies are overwhelming and conclusive that a person's self-concept is easily reshaped with this technique. Persons with low self-esteem will do a lot of things, but giving up who they are and how they see themselves is not one of them.

PHASE 3: GET HIM TO INVEST *IN YOU*

When you ask for his advice or ideas, he gives of himself. He gives his thoughts, time, and attention. When we make an investment in someone or something, we treat it with greater respect. Whether we're talking about a boat, a company, or a person, the psychology is the same. We protect and do not harm what we invest in.

Now you become his biggest supporter, his greatest fan. To turn on you would be like turning on himself—even worse, as you seem to appreciate him *more* than he appreciates himself. (See Chapter 12 for additional helpful techniques.)

REAL-WORLD, REAL-LIFE EXAMPLE AND SCENARIO

SCENARIO: A restaurant manager always yells at the waiter for the littlest things.

> **WAITER:** [at a quiet, nonhectic time, when they are casually talking] *"You know what I respect very much about you, Mr. Harris? You always seem to be so calm and cool under such pressure, I find that so amazing."*
> **MR. HARRIS:** *"Well, I do lose my temper sometimes."*
> **WAITER:** *"Yes, I guess everyone does. You just seem to be in control more than most."*

Mr. Harris now sees himself through the eyes of the waiter. The next time he feels compelled to yell at the waiter, he stops himself—mostly unconsciously—because he doesn't want to shatter the image of himself as someone in control.

In addition to this, the waiter asks, at another time, for advice.

> *"Mr. Harris, I know that you're a real worldly kind of guy. It's kind of personal, but I'd really like to know if I can get your advice on a problem I've been having with my girlfriend."*

You see, as soon as the manager eagerly offers his advice, he will have made an emotional investment in the waiter. And as with any type of investment, we care what happens to it. We don't abuse it or injure it. Mr. Harris will no longer be yelling at this waiter.

✳ FLASH REVIEW ✳

You can cool off any hothead by doing three things: (1) Establish mutual respect, (2) reshape her self-concept so she sees herself as a different person—which forces her to behave differently, and (3) get her to make an emotional investment in you.

CHAPTER 12

SPECIAL TECHNIQUES FOR SPECIAL PEOPLE: FROM NEUROTIC TO PSYCHOTIC, GETTING ALONG WITH PEOPLE WHO ARE EMOTIONALLY UNWELL

If you are dealing with individuals who are a little "off" or who suffer from mental illness, it will help you to know that they *all* crave the very same thing: peace of mind. Their thoughts have become chaotic. They don't feel in control of themselves and their lives. From obsessive thoughts to constant worry, they are always on edge, never feeling grounded.

The techniques you use will infuse these persons with a sense of stability and independence. While you will probably not cure them by changing how you relate to them, you will greatly enhance your ability to enjoy the best-quality relationship possible.

STRATEGIC PSYCHOLOGICAL SOLUTION

This person typically tries to engage in a lifestyle that is free of stress, as stress adds to the inner turmoil. The problem with that is when a person tries to remove stress from his life, by doing less, more stress is actually added. The further a person moves away from his world, the further he moves away from reality. He then becomes more unstable as he has less information by which to make decisions and feels out of touch. His thinking becomes rigid and his perspective black-and-white.

Of course, much of your approach and interaction depends on where he or she is emotionally and your relationship. As we are dealing with a multitude of variables, these are some solid psychological tools to build the best relationship you can.

PHASE 1: MAKE HER FEEL SPECIAL

This helps shore up her feeling of helplessness and is accomplished by doing a few very simple things:

- Show enthusiasm for being around her. If she gets the impression that it is a chore for you to have a conversation with her, it will eat away at her self-esteem and the bond between you.
- Show appreciation for her ideas and her time. When you speak with her, give your full time and attention to the conversation. And be diligent in thanking her for her opinions and ideas whether or not you agree with them.
- Be attentive to her needs and comfort. Even something simple such as getting her a glass of water if she seems thirsty goes miles in making her feel good about herself and her relationship with you.

PHASE 2: DEMONSTRATE TRUST

Someone who is unbalanced often doesn't trust herself and her own judgment. When you show that you trust her, she regains a sense of worth and confidence in herself.

- Ask for her advice and input. Get her opinion on things. It gives her a chance to give, and this helps her to feel self-reliant.
- Have her help you with a project or assignment. Solicit her help to give her a chance to contribute to something and someone else. Instability often creates a mode of self-absorption and sometimes narcissistic behavior. Taking the focus off herself and her own problems gives her a healthier perspective.

PHASE 3: INSTILL A SENSE OF INDEPENDENCE

Help her to feel a sense of control and freedom in what she does and how she lives her life.

- If the situation allows, let her be in charge as much as possible of her own life. Sometimes we want to help this person to alleviate unnecessary stress, but in doing so we create a larger sense of dependency. Give her the ability to be in charge of herself as much as you can.
- Ask her to do something and give her full autonomy in its planning and execution—from beginning to end.

TWO MAIN PROBLEM AREAS

1. Handling criticism: Sometime this person can be hypercritical and this can be the cause of much friction between you. (Please see Chapters 5, 8, and 11 for great techniques on simply and easily handling criticism and unwanted advice.)

2. Setting boundaries: You will do her no good by letting her have free range. While allowing her a degree of freedom is beneficial, it's important to set up a structure and appropriate parameters to keep you from being either a verbal punching bag or being driven nuts by her erratic behavior. Whether it's dropping by without calling or asking you about something private, you need to lay down the law . . . gently. (Please see Chapter 9 on how best to accomplish this. See Chapter 11 for other helpful techniques.)

REAL-WORLD, REAL-LIFE EXAMPLE AND SCENARIO

SCENARIO: Jill has an aunt who is unwell. Whenever they get together, Jill is always on edge and uncomfortable, because her aunt has a habit of making rude remarks and asking inappropriate questions.

JILL: [upon seeing her aunt, she shows genuine enthusiasm, and when speaking to her, she gives her full attention and is attentive to her aunt's moods] *"Aunt Harriet, I was wondering if you could help*

*me with something. I've been thinking about redoing the kids' room
and you have such a flair for decorating. Do you think you could
swing by one day next week and look at some furniture with me?"*

Her aunt is naturally flattered and feels good that Jill has sought out
her opinion. Jill follows up after the aunt has helped.

*"You know, Aunt Harriet, you've been such a big help, thank you.
I'm wondering if I could impose on you once more. We're having a
party for John's boss in a few weeks. Do you think you might have
time to plan the menu? I'll leave it in your very capable hands."*

You see, when you give someone the chance to do something for
someone else and give to you, it makes that person feel good. It is best,
too, to seek out this person's advice and help with something that will
not cause it to be the end of the world if things don't go the way you
had hoped. And after a short time you will find that she treats you entirely differently.

✳ FLASH REVIEW ✳

You can improve your relationship with anyone who is emotionally
unstable by (1) making her feel important and appreciated, (2)
showing that you trust her, and (3) giving her an increased sense of
responsibility and freedom.

SECTION II

PUTTING OUT SMALL FIRES: RESOLVE SIMPLE
DISAGREEMENTS AND ARGUMENTS IN YOUR FAVOR
WHEN YOU GET ANYONE TO SEE THE SITUATION
FROM YOUR POINT OF VIEW

If you're tired of arguing over the same old things time and again, now you can get anyone to see and agree—happily!—with your point of view. In any relationship or situation, you can eliminate all of those annoying quarrels once and for all.

Whether you want someone to do something or you want him to back off from his demands, you can do it fast and easy. And for those times when you both want what's best but disagree over how to proceed, get your way—right away—without an argument and barely a conversation!

Remember, relationships are built on trust, honesty, and respect, so make sure your motivations are good and the benefits to all parties are clear. Please see "A Note to Readers" (page xv) for further clarification of this necessity.

CHAPTER 13

GET ANYONE *TO DO* OR *NOT DO* SOMETHING, HAPPILY AND
WITHOUT AN ARGUMENT

Every time you bring it up, there's an argument. But it's driving you crazy. You want someone to do or not do something, and he's not cooperating. He either doesn't see your point, doesn't care enough to, or simply isn't interested in listening.

In any case, if it is not a matter of life and death, you can gain immediate cooperation if you (a) establish or reestablish respect in the relationship and (b) employ specific techniques to influence behavior.

STRATEGIC PSYCHOLOGICAL SOLUTION

PHASE 1: THREE STAGES TO ESTABLISH MUTUAL RESPECT

> The following three-stage process gives *core techniques*—part of an overall psychological strategy—and applies to Chapter 14 as well. To avoid redundancy, they are explained here and are referred to by name only in the solution section of Chapter 14.

Laying the groundwork by establishing greater respect is the key part of your strategy. Lack of respect is the basis for your lack of cooperation and at the crux of the solution. There are three highly effective methods to accelerate and establish mutual respect.

1. Ask her opinion. Seek her input, thoughts, or suggestion on something unrelated. The smartest person we know is the one who asks for our advice. Additionally, when someone gives you advice, she makes an emotional investment in you, and so is more willing to go out of her way to make you happy.

2. Tell a third person what you respect and admire about her. Or if more appropriate in personal situations, tell someone how much you like what she's done or the way she does something—cooks, works, fixes things, does crafts, whatever. When we find out that someone thinks well of us, we are again inclined to alter our feelings toward this person—at both the unconscious and the conscious level.

Additionally, studies prove, and life experience shows, that we are more likely to *respect* someone who has respect for us. Alternatively, if we feel that someone does not respect us, then we have to alter our perception of him to something less flattering. Why? Because we must unconsciously resolve to conclude that he is not a good person and not worthy of our respect, as the only other option is that this great person doesn't respect me, so there must be something wrong with me. It's much gentler on our psyche to reevaluate our opinion of him.

3. Give a small gift of appreciation. When you bring someone a gift or do something nice for him because you want him to forgive you for something you did, it's sometimes not received in the best way because *you had to do it,* it was expected. *You are doing this because you did that.* It's seen as an obligation on your part. But when you do something to show your *appreciation* for something someone did for you, then this is truly a sign of respect. Notice, though, that you should not give a gift as a *reward* for someone's behavior. However, a sign of appreciation for something unrelated is very effective.

We do the three stages in Phase 1 for this reason. You want to make sure that her behavior is not due to her feeling that she's not getting enough respect from you. The fact is, if she resents the way you've been treating her, when it comes to specific instances, like this one, she may adopt a hard stance merely because she wants to assert herself. By engaging in mutual respect, you are able to remove this obstacle from the equation and tip success in your favor.

PHASE 2: LEADING BY EXAMPLE

If you want someone to do something, lead by example if it is practical to do so. (There are few things more annoying than someone who barks out orders yet refuses to take his own advice.) This engages a psychological law called *social proof,* which basically says that we look to others for cues on what is appropriate behavior in a given situation. Studies conclude that if he sees you doing what you want him to do or even hears about others in similar situations doing the same thing, he will be unconsciously driven to do the same.

PHASE 3: POSITIVE REINFORCEMENT

When he does what you want, encourage him further with positive words, feedback, encouragement, and appreciation. But *do not* reward his behavior with anything other than verbal appreciation and praise. Research in human behavior concludes that when we are given an external justification for our actions—money or any type of compensation—our desire to repeat this behavior is lessened. This is because we perceive the reward as our motivation and lose internal desire. That is why the quickest way to discourage a child from doing something good is to reward him or her with anything other than praise. Payment takes the wind out of our sails, as we are no longer able to maintain that we did good because we are good people. Cults are in part so effective because they never create any real tangible external justification. Therefore, new members need to rationalize their behavior by adjusting their thinking to *I must really believe in this cause, because why else would I be doing this? I'm not getting a sports car. And I don't even look good with my head shaved!*

PHASE 4: EMPLOY NEGATIVE ASSOCIATION

This technique comes courtesy of Russian scientist Ivan Pavlov. In short, in the course of an unrelated experiment, he noticed that the dogs he was working with salivated when he walked into the room. They had learned that seeing Pavlov meant that they would be fed. And even without the food, they salivated because they *associated* Pavlov to the food. This is what's called a conditioned reflex, and we can see examples of it in our own lives.

For instance, perhaps the smell of tequila makes you nauseous because you had a "bad experience" with it several years ago. Or a certain song comes on the radio and it reminds you of a friend you haven't thought about in years. These are all anchors. An anchor is an association or link between a specific set of feelings or an emotional state and some unique stimulus—an image, sound, name, or taste.

When someone associates his actions with unpleasant stimuli, he will begin to form an unconscious link and get a negative feeling from what was once pleasurable. Here's how it's done. When a person is doing something you don't like, you need to *anchor* this event with a negative association. You can do this in a variety of ways: by reminding him that his actions are causing you pain, or by letting him know that you are disappointed when he engages in this behavior. In a short time he will develop a negative association with this particular action. (Please see Chapter 14 for other helpful techniques.)

CAN YOU PUT GLOVES ON PLEASE?

How do you *remind* someone to do something when you know that the mere act of *asking* is going to offend him? The all-time best technique is to tell the person that *you don't mind if he does it*. For instance, let's say that you're in a deli and the person behind the counter is not wearing gloves. He's handling money and wiping up the floor. Now he's about to make your sandwich. Asking him to please put gloves on shouldn't be offensive, but if you are concerned about his taking offense you would merely say, "Oh, you don't need to put gloves on if you don't want to." In which case he will probably put them on, as he wasn't "told to," but he knows that he is supposed to.

This is also similar to the reason why flight attendants will ask you to "take your seat" rather than telling you to "sit down." Asking you to take your seat doesn't make you defensive, as the request puts you in charge—*you* are going to *take your seat*. Telling you to sit down puts her in charge. This subtle difference in the language makes a major impact on how we internalize the request.

REAL-WORLD, REAL-LIFE EXAMPLE AND SCENARIO

SCENARIO: Beth wants her mother-in-law, Louise, to stop gossiping to her about everybody and everything.

> **BETH:** *"Louise, you always make the best tuna casserole. Can you give me the recipe so I can make it for dinner this week?"*

Louise happily obliges. After making the meal, Beth tells a few people that the recipe was her mother-in-law's and that she is just the best cook around. She then picks up a small gift of appreciation.

> *"I know it was no big deal for you, but it felt so good to get such compliments on my cooking. I saw this in the store and thought you would like it, and I just wanted to say thank you."*

Beth makes a point of refraining from gossiping herself in order to lead by example. She also gives positive reinforcement to Louise, even when there is only a thin reason to do so, as follows.

> [A day or so later] *"Louise, I know that you were going to tell me about X and didn't because you know how much I don't like gossiping. I want you to know I truly appreciate your stopping yourself."*

Even though Louise may have had no intention of saying anything, the positive feedback will go a long way to curbing her behavior. And should she "slip," Beth will offer a negative association to further keep her mother-in-law's behavior in line.

> *"I don't know if you realize how much it hurts me and our relationship when you gossip. You have such a great mind, you should use it for thinking about better things than gossip."*

✷ FLASH REVIEW ✷

Getting someone to do it your way is easy when you use a psychological strategy that combines establishing respect, using positive reinforcement, using negative association, and engaging the law of social proof by leading by example.

CHAPTER 14

WHEN YOU BOTH WANT WHAT'S BEST BUT DISAGREE OVER HOW TO PROCEED, GET YOUR WAY, RIGHT AWAY

This strategy is for those times when there's a difference of opinion on how to best accomplish something—disciplining children, running the office, decorating, and so on. These are situations involving preference, opinion, and matters of approach and taste. There is no readily obvious objective truth, and each person feels he is correct, from his own perspective. When both of you want to accomplish the same objective but just disagree on how best to proceed, use this psychological strategy to resolve your conflict fast and easy.

STRATEGIC PSYCHOLOGICAL SOLUTION

Even though we have a difference of opinion, the reason that it becomes a problem has to do with respect.

If the person with whom you disagree believed that you had *full and complete* respect for him, then he would never make an issue out of something minor. The reality is that no one ever argues over socks on the floor, what color to paint the kitchen, or where to eat. We argue over the right to be heard, the right to have our beliefs validated, and the right to be who we are. So if she knows that you appreciate and respect her, she won't always feel the need to assert herself in these other ways. If you try to argue about why you are right, you may win the battle but lose the proverbial war, because the next time an issue comes up she will be even more adamant, as she will feel even less respected in the relationship. So if you go to the root, to the source, and fix that, then any confrontations that would stem from it will be no more.

The reality is that sometimes a person is more interested in being right than in doing what is right, meaning that he wants to do it his way and prove that he's the smart one, even at the expense of an ideal outcome. Therefore, when you show the person that you do accept and appreciate him, his focus naturally shifts to what is really important. And that is doing what is best for the relationship, rather than trying to show who is in charge.

PHASE 1: THREE STAGES TO ESTABLISH MUTUAL RESPECT

Please go to Chapter 13, page 58, for a detailed illustration of the following three-stage process:

1. *Ask his opinion.*
2. *Tell a third person how much you respect and admire him.*
3. *Give a small gift of appreciation.*

PHASE 2: RECIPROCAL PERSUASION: YOU SCRATCH MY BACK, I'LL SCRATCH YOURS

Psychologist Robert Cialdini introduced a principle in psychology called reciprocal persuasion, which says if you change your mind about something because I ask you to, then when you ask me to change my mind about something, I'm more likely to do it.

So if you let a person know that you changed your mind because of something that he had suggested to you, then he will be more likely to change his mind because of you. In addition to invoking the law of reciprocal persuasion, you do another very other powerful thing. You show, by taking his advice, that you *trust* his judgment and value his input.

METS OR YANKEES?

If you're arguing over something specific and objective, such as who won the 1928 World Series, then *go find out!* Go to an objective, respectable source and get the answer. Whenever you are arguing over specific facts, stop and find a reliable source to verify the answer.

PHASE 3: ADOPT A TWO-SIDED ARGUMENT

Studies show that when a person holds an opposing view, you should adopt a two-sided argument. If you ignore his reasoning, he will believe *you* to be unreasonable. Therefore, present a balanced approach by laying down both sides and arguments for the issue.

PHASE 4: DO ME A FAVOR

Instead of making it an issue about right or wrong, simply *ask him* to do it as a *favor*. Tell him that:

1. You thought about his position—what he wants, does, likes, and so on—and realize how he feels about it.
2. You understand that he doesn't agree with you and that he feels he is right, but you would still like him to go along with your way of thinking.
3. You will do it his way, without hesitation or conversation, if it becomes clear that your way isn't working. And if it's a onetime only situation, then agree to do something else his way if yours doesn't work out for the best.

Now he feels as if he's doing something *nice*—a favor for you—as opposed to giving in. This completely changes the psychological dynamics, because he can still be right, not change his thinking, *and do it anyway*.

Often we're so consumed with making our point and winning the argument that we lose sight of what we really want—and that's having the other person do what we want. Additionally, it's win-win, since if he wants what is best, he will get to do it his way right away should your way not work.

REAL-WORLD, REAL-LIFE EXAMPLE AND SCENARIO

SCENARIO: We'll use a *generic* script here, so plug in husband, boss, friend, child, neighbor—anyone, in any circumstance.

"Richard, I'd like to get your thoughts on X."

A few days later or whenever appropriate, bring a small gift.

"I just want you to know that I took your advice, and you were right about X, it worked out great. I really appreciate your taking the time to help me with it. I told Andy all about it, too."

Should you happen to see or speak with him afterward, remember to thank him again.

"I was going to go an entirely different way, but I'm glad you talked to me about doing it the other way. You could not have been more right."

At various times, and wherever possible, you are reinforcing positive behavior with praise and discouraging negative behavior. Additionally, you fold into your praise the technique for reshaping the self-concept.

You've laid the groundwork and given respect so this person will now be (a) able to and (b) eager to show respect to you and for your opinions.

[Then, when he's in a fairly good mood] *"By the way, regarding X? I know that you believe your way is less expensive/ proven/better in the long run, but do you think it's possible for us to* [however you want it to be done]. *I'd really like for us to try it this way. It would mean a lot to me."*

You will be amazed at how easy this is.

> ✳ **FLASH REVIEW** ✳
>
> Even though we have a difference of opinion, the reason that it becomes a conflict has to do with each person seeing things from a fixed perspective. No one argues over "things." It's always about principles and values and the right to be heard. Initiate a five-phase process to increase respect and engage reciprocal persuasion. Adopt a two-sided argument. Then simply ask for what you want.

CHAPTER 15

"Two for Me, and None for You":
The Best Method to Divide Anything
Fairly and Equitably to Avoid a Conflict

What should we do with those people who always think that they're being taken advantage of? They just don't seem to have a sense about what is equitable and see the world only through their jilted glasses. Whether it's who pays what, who gets what, or who did what, they always think they're getting the raw end of the deal.

These people usually suffer from low self-esteem and have a skewed *sense of fairness.* And that is for two reasons. One is that they are focused on immediate gratification, because they don't like who they are and need to constantly seek comfort and/or enjoyment in order to feel good. Anything that pulls them away from this causes an emotional upheaval. Second, they can't readily see circumstances from another's point of view.

That's what being self-centered is—seeing things as if you were the center of the universe. In his book, *Prisoners of Hate,* Aaron Beck writes, "Depressed patients often relate irrelevant events as a sign of their own unworthiness or imperfections." His findings effectively illustrate the idea that these people have a warped perspective and understanding of their world and those in it.

STRATEGIC PSYCHOLOGICAL SOLUTION

From who does what to who gets what to where you go, use these strategies to quickly resolve any division of property, or argument over who is supposed to do what when. (If you simply want this person to do a specific thing, then go to Chapter 13 and use those techniques to get your way.)

Before we apply specific techniques, it's important to know that each and every conflict has two main ingredients: *ego* and the *facts*. It's important to address both of these factors. You will see that when you do so, almost any conflict can be effectively and easily resolved. While this may seem like an oversimplification, the process addresses those key points offering a fast, comprehensive, and thorough solution to almost any situation of this type.

To address the ego, we need to make sure that the person is not holding his ground—being unreasonable or stubborn—merely because he is looking for respect. I cannot stress this enough. Treat the other party with complete respect and you will find that regardless of how he treats you, you will overcome this obstacle. (For further clarification and examples of how to introduce respect into the dynamics, please see Chapters 12 and 13.)

Once you've taken care of the issue of respect, you can plug various options into your situation, depending on the nature of the conflict:

SOLUTION 1: YOU DIVIDE, I PICK

One party divides the items into two "piles" and the other party picks which one he wants. This is one of the oldest and most equitable ways to distribute or divide anything. It provides a checks-and-balances situation whereby each side is able to assert its demands. (Note: More advanced concepts and strategies for use in high-stakes situations—such as negotiation, mediation, and arbitration—are found in Chapter 25.)

Now, if there is only *one item* that both people want, then each person puts into the virtual pile those things he is willing to give up in order to gain this one item. After that is done, the technique is the same—one person divides and the other picks.

SOLUTION 2: YOU, ME, ME, YOU

Another universally fair method is to alternate choosing, with one person going first, then the second party having two picks. It then alternates again evenly, with one pick per party, back and forth until all the items have been selected.

SOLUTION 3: IT'S YOUR TURN! NO, IT'S MINE! FINE, I LEAVE IT UP TO YOU

This is a great technique anytime you are arguing over who is supposed to do what when. Because so much of the conflict is a psychological power struggle, if you give the person your "power," you will find that he often becomes *more* fair and empathetic to your cause.

The idea of giving someone power is well illustrated in this story. A good friend of mine is the head fund-raiser for a large nonprofit organization. Each day he asks people for hundreds of thousands, sometimes millions of dollars. Occasionally, he will go back to the same donor—someone who just gave money a mere month ago—and ask for another donation. While some people think that this is an insane practice, he continually develops great relationships with these donors. What's his secret to avoid offending them?

Simple. He doesn't ask for another donation. Instead *he asks if he can ask* for a donation. Do you see the difference in the dynamics? If he were to ask for money outright, he would put the person on the defensive and risk coming across as ungrateful—this creates a power struggle. But by *asking if he can ask,* he puts the person in a position of power and control and as such eliminates his defenses. Why? Because she can simply say no to the question, and does not have to say no to the request for money.

Another application of this psychology was used by a very savvy woman while speaking to a large crowd on a controversial subject. Her colleague, during his presentation, had been subjected to yelling, screaming, and booing. He walked off the stage in the middle of his talk. Now it was her turn to face the mob. She walked to the podium and said the following: "You were all very rude to Frank and that made him angry. If you are like that to me, you are going to make me cry." She got a smattering of laughter from that line and then spoke for nearly forty minutes, *uninterrupted.*

She managed to completely disarm the audience. What's going on in the mind of the listeners? What would there be to gain by making a grown woman cry? Nothing. They had won the power struggle. Yes, they could make her cry if they wanted to. Okay. Let's hear what she has to say. We still have power over her. She told us that much herself.

Therefore, tell the person that you believe him to be fair and reasonable and that you will abide by his decision. (If it's absurd, you can always argue that he is being too unfair.) But you will find, often, that *once he has control,* he has no need to assert his power and will probably be fair and balanced in his decision. This is true also because if he's negotiating for something, he wants to get the best deal. "I won" will be what he wants to think to himself afterward. But when we're in charge of a situation, we often seek to do what is fair and right because there is no psychological gain to getting "more." It's up to us anyway. This approach completely locks the ego out of the decision-making process. Of course, it helps if you're dealing with someone who is somewhat reasonable. If this is not the case, then please see Chapter 25 to best accomplish your objective.

REAL-WORLD, REAL-LIFE EXAMPLE AND SCENARIO

SCENARIO A: Two workers are arguing over who gets the bigger office.

Solution 1: Since there's only one office, other items such as parking space, nicer chair, and oak desk are thrown into the mix. One person divides everything into what he believes are two equal "piles." The other person is then asked to pick whichever collection he wants. He may not choose the group with the office, opting instead to have some of the other items. The one who divided the piles may get the office in exchange for what he considers to be a fair trade—the items in the pile that the other person chose.

SCENARIO B: Two children are arguing over who gets what toys that were given to them to "share" for the holidays.

Solution 2: All the toys are either listed or in front of each child. They alternate picking a toy to be placed into their pile, until all of the toys are gone (or broken).

SCENARIO C: John, wants his friend to pay for some of the repairs to his car that were incurred when they took a cross-country road trip.

Solution 3: JOHN: *"Bill, you know what? We're good friends and I don't want this to hurt our relationship. I know that you're a fair guy, and maybe I'm not seeing this right. I want to leave it up to you. You just give me a check for what you think is fair, and that will be fine."*
  Now there's no winning for Bill, as he can get whatever he wants. By giving him control, *you take away his opportunity to win anything.* Now when he does what is right, he feels as if he is doing it because he's a good person and not because he has to or because he lost the argument.

✳ FLASH REVIEW ✳

Most simple arguments over what is right and fair can be settled by first eliminating interference by the egos and then using any one of a variety of methods for equal distribution. Additionally, the tactic of relinquishing your control to the other party gives you a unique psychological advantage that eliminates his need to try to get the better of you.

SECTION III

WHEN YOU MESS UP A LITTLE: THE PSYCHOLOGICAL SECRETS TO QUICKLY AND EASILY GAIN FORGIVENESS

In seconds, you can erase in the mind of anyone, anything you said or did that caused embarrassment, resentment, or hurt feelings. When you are misunderstood, misspeak, or act without thinking, use these psychological strategies to set things right. If you deeply regret your mistake then get your relationship back on track fast.

> Remember, relationships are built on trust, honesty, and respect, so make sure your motivations are good and the benefits to all parties are clear. Please see "A Note to Readers" (page xv) for further clarification of this necessity.

CHAPTER 16

"You Called Me a *What*?": When You *Say* the Wrong Thing, Make It Okay in Less Than One Minute

Over the centuries, one of the oldest and most important questions that military leaders have asked is *What is the best way to minimize casualties if you are ambushed—suddenly attacked by the enemy?* Do you wait and plan a strategy? Call in reinforcements? Retreat? Most military experts have concluded that the most effective response is often to *throw down cover fire and charge your enemy right away and as fast as you can!*

It's true that time is the great healer, but time can also *solidify* ill feelings as well. Therefore, your best approach is to reduce as much of the initial damage as quickly as you can. Charge up the hill and deal with it fast. Letting it play out can often cause the situation to fester and grow to become a larger problem, as the person holding the grudge will begin to think of all the "other things" that you've done and justify to herself that you are not the kind of person she thought you to be. You want to get *in* and get *out* before this spark becomes a psychological fire.

"YOU SAID *WHAT* BEHIND MY BACK?"

If your words get twisted or you unintentionally offend someone when speaking to a third party, dilute the impact fast. For instance, "No, I didn't say *you* were driving me crazy. I said *everyone* was driving me crazy." Since she's hearing it third-hand, there's usually enough doubt to throw you into the clear. The difference in the psychological dynamics is that between having someone in the office walk up to you and give you the finger and say "I hate you," and having the same person walk into a room of people and do the same thing to everyone. The impact is diffused. And this can be done after the fact, by simply globalizing what you say—making it about more than just her.

STRATEGIC PSYCHOLOGICAL SOLUTION

PHASE 1: DEPERSONALIZE THE IMPACT

Put your statement within the context of a larger point in order to dilute it. For example, "It's not that I don't like *your* fish sandwich, I just don't like fish, period." If she doesn't take it personally, then she can't be offended. By reducing the personal impact of your comment you take most of the sting out of it.

PHASE 2: APOLOGIZE AND TAKE THE BLAME

You say that you are sorry *after* the first step instead of right away. The reason is that if you apologize first, it means that you are sorry for *saying* what you did. But it doesn't convey that what you said was not what you meant. When you shift the apology to after your "disclaimer," it's heard in a better light. The apology also includes a statement to reduce the impact, by showing that *you* are the one who is off, not the other person.

PHASE 3: DO A CASUAL FOLLOW-UP

Without making a big deal out of it, speak to the person in private about how you "lost it." If possible, throw in something personal to show that you trust her and, if you like, ask for her advice if she doesn't offer it.

REAL-WORLD, REAL-LIFE EXAMPLE AND SCENARIO

SCENARIO: A boss tells her assistant that he is completely incompetent in front of a room full of people.

> **BOSS:** *"Steve, you screwed up that account incredibly. How stupid are you?"* [The boss, realizing that she spoke too harshly, then says] *"All of you and everyone in shipping are screwing up left and right. Can't anyone do anything right around here? You know I expect more from you than everybody else."*
>
> [Pause] *"You know what, everyone? I'm sorry, I'm just not myself today. I'm really annoyed about something else, not you. This is the third time I lost my temper today."*
>
> [Later that day] *"You know, Steve, I think I need a vacation. I've been so edgy lately."*

Now the boss has managed to avoid having Steve take the full impact from what she said and everyone else thinks that the boss is a big person for admitting she was wrong and apologizing for it publicly. She succeeds at extracting the proverbial win-win out of a losing situation.

❋ FLASH REVIEW ❋

You can recover quickly when you speak without thinking by employing a three-phase process where you (1) dilute the impact, (2) take responsibility, and (3) follow up with a vulnerable "confession."

CHAPTER 17

GAIN FORGIVENESS: WHEN YOU DO THE WRONG THING AND
IT *CAN* BE CORRECTED, AND WHEN YOU DO THE WRONG
THING AND IT *CANNOT* BE CORRECTED

These techniques are for the times when you made a mistake with something that can be fixed, repaired, or replaced. You can make restitution, but you were in the wrong and want to make things okay between the two of you as well as do the right thing.

A strategy is also provided for times when you can't fix the exact mistake, such as when you forgot an anniversary or a birthday, or gave someone bad advice, use these techniques to smooth things over and get your relationship back on track, fast.

STRATEGIC PSYCHOLOGICAL SOLUTION

PHASE 1: APOLOGIZE

Here you want to apologize first and fast, because there is no getting around that you were in the wrong. If you leave an apology out, and don't actually say the words that you are sorry, the person is going to have a hard time forgiving you. *So say it.* Another thing to keep in mind is that your apology should be sincere. If you don't mean it, don't say it.

PHASE 2: DEPERSONALIZE IMPACT

Place your actions within a larger context—one that caused you personal harm or pain (if true, of course)—so that your behavior is diluted.

For instance, "Not only did I forget to call when I got back, but I forgot that I was supposed to meet my boss at the office."

PHASE 3: SOLIDIFY IN THE REAL WORLD

Take actual, concrete steps to assure her that your actions will not be *repeated,* or *begin now* to repair any damage if the situation *can* be fixed.

PHASES 1, 2, AND 3 PLUS . . .

CAN BE CORRECTED

PHASE 4A: BETTER THAN NEW

Try to make it better than it was before to show true regret and remorse. And most important, get moving with it *before* you even tell her about it.

PHASE 5A: EMPHASIZE RESPECT

Try to give a reason for the damage that does not show carelessness or a lack of respect on your end. If you were being responsible in your actions and something unforeseen beyond your control interfered, then she will clearly be less annoyed than if you acted with casual disregard.

CANNOT BE CORRECTED

PHASE 4B: ALTERNATIVE REALITY

If you can offer a motivation that depicts you as *trying* to do something nice that simply backfired, all the better. For instance, a long time ago you planned something for her birthday because you wanted it to be just right, but in the time that has passed they misplaced your deposit.

PHASE 5B: RESTORE BALANCE

By putting effort—time, money, energy, *without a guarantee of success*—into the relationship, you help bring it into balance. This can be done in either of two ways: One is an actual investment of yourself. The second is a declaration that it has been bothering you, because if you continue to suffer guilt and anguish, balance is also restored.

REAL-WORLD, REAL-LIFE EXAMPLE AND SCENARIO

But hold on . . . before we begin, if he's raging, *just listen.* Don't comment, disagree, or argue. Sometimes the person just needs to get it off his chest, so let him speak. Other times he's looking for a fight. If you don't interrupt, he will run out of things to say. Do not get defensive or you will get an argument. If there are extenuating circumstances, save it for later. Now is not the time for what may be seen as an excuse. The exception here is something that would *completely exonerate* you— this you can share right away. Okay, now on to business. . . .

SCENARIO A [cannot be corrected]: Fran, who organized the event, never invited her sister-in-law to the family reunion.

> FRAN: *"I am so sorry. I heard six other people were also never invited. But it's all my fault, because I said I wanted to call you myself so we would have a chance to catch up beforehand. I so missed talking to you. I keep playing it over and over again in my mind about how this could have happened. I feel so terrible and it just wasn't the same without you. I'm never going to let this happen again.*
>
> *You know what? Let's get together, just the two of us. It would be a great way to spend some time and talk about the old days with you. Do you want to check your schedule now to see if we*

can pick a date? I'm flexible, so whatever is good for you, is good for me."

SCENARIO B [cannot be corrected]: Jim was three hours late for dinner and didn't call his wife.

JIM: *"I am so sorry, honey. Not only didn't I call you, but I never called back a major client. We got caught up in the meeting and I wanted to call you when I had an exact time when I'd be home, to see if you wanted to catch a movie. And then before I realized it, it was so late. Let's go now and get a beeper for me, so you can page me whenever you need to. Because I don't want this to happen again. And tomorrow, I'll take off work early if you'll let me cook dinner for you."*

SCENARIO C [can be corrected]: Sam borrowed George's car and dented it.

SAM: *"I'm very sorry about the car. Nothing was going right that day. It got dented because I didn't want to give it to the valet because I know how much you love your car. So when I parked it myself, on the street, that's when it got hit.*

"I've already called several places and gotten quotes. I'll take care of it anyway you want. You can either give me the insurance information, or I can give you the quotes I got. Also I'm going to have them detail the entire car so it will look like new. That's on me. I just feel so badly about this happening."

You see how doing it this way, instead of offering a lame excuse and a quick apology, makes the person feel appreciated so she can't help but be more understanding.

Note: If you haven't been able to shut down the conflict, then you may have underestimated the damage done. So proceed to Chapter 18 to ensure success. Before you do, though, try this lifesaving phrase: *"I need to make this right. You are too important to me. What must I say or do to make this right between us?"* Then do it.

WHATEVER YOU DO . . .

Do not say, "What's the big deal?" or "How can you be so upset over this?" You want to *empathize* with her, by saying something such as, "I understand why you are so upset." This diffuses the situation and brings balance; by minimizing the situation, you minimize her feelings, and this will only enrage her more.

✳ FLASH REVIEW ✳

Studies show that by shifting a person's perspective, you can minimize the damage of any minor transgression. Approaches include: (1) depersonalizing the impact, (2) shifting your intention, (3) solidifying your commitment to change, and (4) restoring balance to the relationship.

SECTION IV

When You Mess Up a Lot: Learn the Complete Psychological Strategy to Get Anyone to Forgive You for Anything: Whether You Lied, Cheated, or Stole, You Can Make Things Right Again, Fast

This is for more serious transgressions, where one person has done something that is objectively wrong. Whether or not considerable time has passed, there is little or no contact and the person has thus far not forgiven you.

Cheated ~ Lied ~ Betrayed ~ Stole ~ Violation of Trust

Remember, relationships are built on trust, honesty, and respect, so make sure your motivations are good and the benefits to all parties are clear. Please see "A Note to Readers" (page xv) for further clarification of this necessity.

CHAPTER 18

GET ANYONE TO FORGIVE YOU FOR ANYTHING:
REESTABLISH ANY FRIENDSHIP OR RELATIONSHIP WHEN YOU
ARE CLEARLY IN THE WRONG: THERE'S SOME INTERACTION,
BUT NO REAL COMMUNICATION

In circumstances like these, where one person has clearly violated the respect, trust, and rights of another, restoring balance to the person's psyche is the primary focus. This is accomplished by employing an easy-to-use but synergistic and intricate psychological strategy encompassing a ten-phase process.

STRATEGIC PSYCHOLOGICAL SOLUTION

Ten Phases to Making Peace. This easy step-by-step system is designed to help you gain forgiveness and establish peace in any situation faster than you could ever imagine.

OVERVIEW

Phase 1. Use the three-star approach.
Phase 2. Accept responsibility.
Phase 3. Apologize sincerely.
Phase 4. Offer a suggestion for consequences.
Phase 5. Solidify in the real world.
Phase 6. Establish mutual respect.
Phase 7. Restore a sense of balance.
Phase 8. Establish peace of mind.

Phase 9. Create an internal justification.

Phase 10. Establish a specific game plan.

PHASE 1: THE THREE-STAR APPROACH: KEY FACTORS — RESPECT, EMOTION, AND HUMILITY

Before you start, you have to approach the situation with the utmost delicacy. You don't want to take any chances because of the serious nature of the situation. So try to follow the strategy exactly as it is laid out.

Have Humility: If you come into the situation with anything other than *complete humility,* you are a goner. What does this mean? Lose your ego. *It's not about you,* it's about her.

Be Emotional: It's been clearly established through numerous studies that you need to arouse emotions in your attempt to have her forgive you. Most of our thinking is emotionally based. We then use logic to justify our actions. If you appeal to someone on a strictly logical basis, you will have little chance of making peace. If you have to manufacture emotions, don't bother. If you are not in pain, then you don't really care, so spare both of you from further aggravation and move on.

Show Respect: As we've seen, respect is at the crux of establishing peace in any situation. Therefore, you need to be certain that you address the person and employ these techniques *while maintaining the highest degree of respect.* This means you should not argue and scream your point, or show up at her office demanding that she listen to your side of the story. It means asking permission before you speak to her and *prior* to initiating contact if the relationship is severely strained. Understand that it is not about what you did as much as it is about the underlying loss of respect. Approaching the situation with respect is essential to your success.

PHASE 2: TAKE FULL RESPONSIBILITY

It is important for you to take full and complete responsibility for your actions. Do not shift blame or assign excuses—this will only exacerbate the situation. She is expecting that you, to some degree, will try to lay off the blame. Placing the blame elsewhere doesn't help, because then only that other thing or person can restore balance. If you take responsibility, then you have the power to set things right. Again, balance must be restored to the relationship in order to reestablish peace.

PHASE 3: SINCERELY APOLOGIZE

Next, apologize for your behavior. Sometimes we forget to actually say the words "I'm sorry." While just these words often aren't enough, they are essential to your overall strategy to gain forgiveness.

Make sure that your sincerity comes across. Any apology that is not sincere will not be believed. And if you are not believed, then you will not be forgiven. If you're truly sorry, then you will not do what you've done again and put this person through more pain. *But if you don't mean it, don't say it.* If you're not truly sorry and remorseful, it might be time to reevaluate the situation, the relationship, and yourself.

> **QUIET ON THE SET!**
> If she's talking, *do not interrupt.* The objective is to restore her sense of control. Give respect to the person, whether or not you respect her point of view. Listen to what she has to say without interrupting. Interrupting shows that you are not willing to let her control the conversation, let alone the situation.

PHASE 4: BE WILLING TO ACCEPT AND EVEN OFFER CONSEQUENCES

A very important phase in this process is to let her know that you are willing to face and accept any and all consequences for your actions. What you did showed a lack of trust and responsibility. Putting yourself in her hands and taking responsibility not just for your actions but for the ensuing consequences goes a long way toward establishing the power that she lost.

It is one thing to talk the talk, but then things can fall apart if she thinks that you are trying to weasel out without accepting any repercussions. Remember your fate (at least with her) rests in her hands at this point anyway. But freely *giving her power*, and acknowledging it as hers to determine the fate of the relationship, is extremely important. She wants justice for what you've done. She wants to be able to exercise her sense of importance. Give her back what you took and you begin to restore balance. You can start by saying something such as, "I know what I did was wrong. You have every right to be angry with me. I'm willing to accept the full consequences of my actions."

THE SUPREME OPINION

Even in court cases, studies show that if you don't show remorse, then you are likely to receive a stiffer sentence. You begin to restore balance with your words or you will be punished as a way of setting things straight. It is in balance that we find justice, and in justice that we find forgiveness. Parenthetically, statistics show that *attractive people* are often given lighter sentences than their aesthetically challenged counterparts. The one exception—where they receive a higher sentence—is if the defendant used his or her looks as a means of committing the crime. For example, inducing someone to commit a crime by coming on to him, or swindling a woman out of her savings.

PHASE 5: SOLIDIFY IN THE REAL WORLD WITH A SPECIFIC ACTION

Actually making a change in your life will go a long way in letting her know that you are sincere in your convictions. *Actions shout, while words whisper.*

Explain to her how the set of circumstances that created this event can never happen again. Part of her disturbance over your behavior is the unpredictability of your actions. That is, it's something that happened and could happen again without notice or warning. If you can assure her that the combination of events can never repeat itself, you will help to alleviate much of her anxiety.

By isolating the event, you minimize its impact on her life as an anomaly, something that she will never have to deal with again. You do this by *making a change in your life* to show that what you did was wrong *AND* you are not making the change merely to be forgiven. Whatever caused the catalyst, *change the dynamics* to prevent or severely minimize the chances of it happening again.

For example, "It will never happen again. I've enrolled in a program for drug addiction." Or "I've told my boss that I won't travel on weekends anymore." Notice we don't say *"I will . . . ,"* because that conveys the message that *I'm trading this for that. I'm changing because I want to be forgiven.* That doesn't show you've changed, only that you're sorry you got caught.

If you state that the action was taken independently of her agreeing to forgive you, she can readily see that you have changed as a person and are not just trying to do what is necessary to make peace. When you take action irrespective of forgiveness, it shows that you know what you did was wrong and this is not quid pro quo. You can also let others know what you have done in making the new change, so that it can filter back to this person.

Phase 6: Reestablish *Mutual* Respect

Do something that shows your true character. Donate money, do charity work, spend time with a sick or elderly person, stand up for someone or for a good cause. *Show her what kind of person you really are.* She needs to respect you again as a person. She's lost respect for you and she's thinking that you may not be the kind of person she thought you to be. It is hard to dislike someone for whom we have great respect. Let her see *your true nature,* so that your transgression is filtered through this better light.

PHASE 7: RESTORE THE SENSE OF BALANCE

It's important to let her know that your actions produced no enjoyment, financial gain, or any type of benefit whatsoever. Since no one can go back in time, you need to explain that not only was it a mistake, it didn't produce the anticipated benefits either. Remember, the key to forgiveness lies in *restoring balance* to the relationship—be it personal or professional. If you gained in some way, then you will have to "give back" more in order to set things right. Never declare any benefits (external rewards) or satisfaction (internal rewards) from your actions. For example, you want to emphasize such truths as, "The experience was lousy," "I never spent any of the stolen money," "I was more miserable and so filled with guilt afterward," and so on.

You have to restore balance any way you can. If you have "it," give it back: money or whatever. If you don't have it but can replace it, do so and make every effort to do so as soon as possible. Let the person know your plan and progress. *And remember, it's important to continue even if she is still not talking to you.* It doesn't end your obligation to do what is right and "repay the debt." This will show your true colors. By continuing to do what is right despite not getting what you want—the relationship back—you will begin to prove yourself to be the kind of person she wants to be involved with or work with, whatever the case may be.

PHASE 8: ESTABLISH PEACE OF MIND

You have to answer the question, Why? Without getting into a long psychological discussion, every wrong action comes down to the *same motivation:* fear. Fear is the henchman of—no surprise—the ego. If you look at what you did, you will find fear at its root.

You stole money, perhaps, because you were scared that you would be at this job for the rest of your life or couldn't give yourself the lifestyle you wanted; you had an affair, perhaps, because you feared that you were unattractive or not lovable. The secret to establishing peace is to find this fear at its source, and to *amplify it.* Stealing money because you like nice things is not as effective a motivation as stealing because you needed to build up a faltering self-image.

Sexual indiscretion, for instance, is not simply an impulse. Fear lurks beneath this action as well. At an unconscious level you may have been thinking, *Is this all there is in life?* Or *Would anyone want to be with me?* Or even a deeper unconscious fear may be, *Things are going too well. I'm not used to this, so let's see how I can mess it up.*

I don't want to get too side-tracked, but let's illustrate this idea with a quick look at the phenomenon that we call a midlife crisis. A person goes out and does all those things that he's feared he missed out on or thinks he will miss. He buys a sports car. Fear. He asks, "What happened to my dreams, my youth? I'm scared." Why doesn't a person commit to marriage? Fear. What if someone better comes along? What if it's a mistake? It all comes back to fear. This is what makes us vulnerable and this is what *you* need to explore, to understand in yourself. Then you need to relate that fear to the person you've hurt.

Now your actions are seen less as a betrayal that violated trust and more as an irrational act of fear by a confused person. It furthers your vulnerability and helps to restore her feeling of power and dignity. By assuaging your fears, she takes an important and active role in restoring her own sense of control.

Rooting your motivations in fear diminishes her perception of your ego. Simply, fear is a response to feelings of your inadequacy to deal with the situation. This is in stark contrast to braggadocio, and a self-centered mind-set—one that you do not want to present.

If you are perceived as the one in control, then *she* is scared and will lash out further. That is why in relationships you rarely find both people jealous of each other. Only one can be. And the other naturally moves to a more comfortable psychological position to strike a balance. Showing fear is readily seen as the shadow of respect. Fear is a sign of recognition of the other person's *power* and *status.* It makes her feel empowered and in control.

After amplifying the fear-based motivation, reestablishing your commitment to the other person and to the relationship is essential. This consists simply of a phrase such as, "You know that our marriage means everything to me and I love you more today then I did when we got married" (if you had an affair). Or "This job has always been the focus of my life; I planned on working here until I retired" (if you stole from your job).

PHASE 9: INTERNAL JUSTIFICATION

Why put things back to the way they were when you can make the relationship *better* than it was?

If you can demonstrate how the relationship will be *better* than it was before the situation, this will be good. Because otherwise, if she agrees to forgive you, she's thinking it's only to go back to a damaged relationship and that may not be worth much to her anymore. No one wants to give up her lifeboat to go back to a sinking ship. But by showing her what happened and the consequent changes you've made to *strengthen* your commitment and relationship, she is gaining something much better than what she lost.

We went through all of that to get to this point. Why throw it away? This is the rationale that makes sense and persuades. And this is accomplished by emphasizing how, by eliminating the cause—the catalyst, as we did in Phase 5—you can make things better than they were before your transgression.

PHASE 10: PUT TOGETHER A SPECIFIC, PAINLESS GAME PLAN

It's important to let her know exactly how things will proceed: slowly, easily, and with her at the controls the entire way. She's thinking, *If I say "okay," it will be hard for me to then kick him out of the house again* (or fire him, or whatever). Therefore, you want to offer a game plan that moves *slowly* but surely toward the objective of reestablishing the relationship. Offer a specific clear-cut course of action for proceeding, making sure that she has the option to, at any time, continue, stop, or change course.

When we are somewhat motivated to take action and move forward, it is essential that we understand the *direction* and the *method* for proceeding. It makes us feel comfortable and secure when we know that the path is clearly lit and laid-out. When you want someone to reconcile, you should provide the desired destination but also the map for getting there.

A SPIRITUAL REFLECTION

Just to cover our bases . . . if you are meeting with resistance, remember that the world is a reflection of you, and *you can only give away what you have*—whether it's love or fear, kindness or anger. And you can only receive what you have, and the only way to have it is to give it away. Got that?

Simply, if you want something to be in your life, you must manifest that quality to some degree. If you want a loving person, you must be a person who loves. Kindness, for example, may exist in the world, but not in *your world,* if you are not kind. The world is set up as a reflection, direct and pure. You cannot receive if you do not give.

Therefore, if you want to be forgiven, you may need to forgive yourself and others. If you are holding on to anger or resentment over what someone has done to you, you can't be sincere with this person. If you can resolve any anger toward yourself or another that you're holding on to, you will find a smoother path ahead in resolving this current situation.

REAL-WORLD, REAL-LIFE EXAMPLE AND SCENARIO

SCENARIO: Jim had a one-night affair. Jim has a drinking problem and often got into heated arguments with his wife, Beth. She has recently learned of her husband's one-night stand.

First he listens and does not raise his voice or interrupt when she is speaking or yelling. He approaches the situation with great humility, emotion, and respect.

"I was completely and utterly wrong. I am deeply, deeply sorry and I regret everything about it. I know what I did was wrong. You have

every right to be angry with me. I'm willing to accept the consequences for my actions.

"Even though I was drinking and don't remember much of what happened, I am fully responsible for putting myself in that situation and for what happened.

"I also want you to know that I've given up drinking completely, and I've already enrolled in a treatment program. I called our insurance to see about coverage for a therapist for me, or if you want, both of us can go, too."

Only if she asks specifically what happened should he proceed to tell her that he got no enjoyment from it—he should not bring this up unless she asks.

"I think maybe, if we are able to work things out, that without my drinking, we won't fight as much about other things. If we can move past this, I think things can be better than they ever were before.

"I don't know how I let this happen. I was scared, but I'm not sure why. [Here he elaborates on possible motivations.] *But I love you and I am committed to doing whatever it takes to make things right and better than they were before.*

"We can go at any pace you want. I'm going over to Al's unless you'll let me sleep here on the couch. Then, after I'm in therapy for a bit, you can tell me what you want to do. [It's important for Jim to end the discussion by putting Beth in charge of the situation.] *Do you want me to leave now?"*

Now he has given her a sense of independence, power, and control over the relationship. The very things that were taken away have been replaced, and he has put her in a psychological position to be willing, able, and eager to give emotionally herself, in the form of forgiving him and making peace.

Furthermore, over the next few weeks or months he will establish himself as someone who is not only redeemable but respectable as well. This is accomplished by him working with people who need his help, showing that he is a caring, giving, good, and respectable person.

"I want you to know, too, that I've decided to work with other people who have addictions."

✳ FLASH REVIEW ✳

You can get anyone to forgive you for anything if you truly regret your actions and commit to not repeating your mistake. This is accomplished by the following ten-phase strategy:

Phase 1. Use the three-star approach.

Phase 2. Accept responsibility.

Phase 3. Apologize sincerely.

Phase 4. Offer a suggestion for consequences.

Phase 5. Solidify in the real world.

Phase 6. Establish mutual respect.

Phase 7. Restore a sense of balance.

Phase 8: Establish peace of mind.

Phase 9. Create an internal justification.

Phase 10. Establish a specific game plan.

CHAPTER 19

BE FORGIVEN WHEN YOU DO SOMETHING CLEARLY
AND OBJECTIVELY WRONG AND THIS PERSON
WANTS *NOTHING* TO DO WITH YOU

The best techniques in the world won't work if you can't get the person to listen to what you have to say. Use these additional techniques in order to be able to use the ones in the previous chapter.

STRATEGIC PSYCHOLOGICAL SOLUTION

Option 1: Restore balance with the jump-start technique.

Option 2: Use Chapter 27 for engaging a third party to help you get this person to listen to what you have to say.

You can use one or both options. Once the person agrees to hear you out, through either option, use the techniques in the previous chapter to make peace.

OPTION 1: RESTORE BALANCE WITH THE JUMP-START TECHNIQUE

In a situation where the person will not even talk to you and/or there has not been any contact for some time, you need to jump-start the relationship by restoring balance. This gets the proverbial psychological ball rolling, *fast*.

If you can make an investment—emotionally, financially, or any other way—and show *effort without progress*, you help to restore balance. You need to put in a great deal of effort by doing something, such as flying to where the person is and dropping off a letter (outlining your feelings and actions as stated in the previous chapter) and then leaving without speaking to the person.

When you do seek her out for a conversation, *ask* to speak with her to *simply apologize*. Then leave. Ask for permission before you do *anything*. Leave right away if she does not want to talk to you and try again another time. (And if you're there only to be yelled at, that's fine, too.) By showing that you put in effort and didn't get anything for it, you help to restore balance, because *she* put effort into the relationship and didn't get what she wanted either.

In our anger we often do the opposite of this and say such things as "I drove all the way here you damn well better talk to me. I said I was sorry! What more do you want?" We show up and speak without permission, and this adds fuel to the flames, as we further demonstrate a lack of respect. This doesn't let the other person feel any sense of control over the situation.

Ninety percent of ending the conflict is in the approach. You almost don't have to say anything as long as you approach the situation with great respect. *Almost.*

Option 2

Use Chapter 27 and employ a third party to help you get the other person to listen to what you have to say. Then use the techniques in the previous chapter.

SECTION V

"THERE'S NO REASON WE SHOULDN'T BE TALKING":
THE SITUATION JUST GOT OUT OF HAND AND NOW
YOU WANT TO MAKE THINGS GOOD AGAIN

When the whole thing just got blown out of proportion and you want to put the pieces back together, do it fast and now. Whether the situation is fresh or time has passed and it's time to let bygones be bygones, put psychology on your side.

Remember, relationships are built on trust, honesty, and respect, so make sure that your motivations are good, and the benefits to all parties are clear. Please see "A Note to Readers" (page xv) for further clarification of this necessity.

CHAPTER 20

"This Is Silly!": When a *Recent* Conversation or Situation Gets Blown Out of Proportion, Smooth Things over Fast and Easy

Even when you are only partly at fault, it is best to approach the person as if you are solely to blame. The reason for this is that if you come in admitting to partial responsibility and he doesn't see things your way, then you are back arguing again.

But after you admit complete blame, you will find that he will then either say, "No, it was my fault, too," or say nothing. After a short time—a week or so—you are welcome to delicately bring up what you think was his role in this, if you feel there is a need to. But you don't want to do this until the two of you have begun to reestablish the bond, as the relationship will be more stable after some time passes.

STRATEGIC PSYCHOLOGICAL SOLUTION

Phase 1: Admit Full Blame

By taking responsibility for yourself and the situation and not blaming him, you pave the way to quickly reignite the relationship. A big mistake we often make is to say something such as, "I got so upset because you did . . ." Or "I didn't think it was a big deal to . . ." Don't blame him for anything—his actions or yours—and don't minimize your role.

Explain to the person that you understand the seriousness of what you did. Do not make light of it. He will naturally take a counter stance. And if you think it necessary, go so far as to *expand* the magnitude of your role. The harder you are on yourself and the more serious you take the situation, the less hard he will be on you. By trying to minimize your role in the conflict, you force him—albeit mostly unconsciously—to go the other way and make it a bigger deal than it was.

PHASE 2: PLEASURE AND PRIDE

Remind the person that you were always proud of him and have had great respect for who he is and how he conducts himself. Say something that conveys your respect, such as "I've always had great respect for you." Or "You know how much I value your opinion and trust your judgment."

PHASE 3: ASK FOR FORGIVENESS

You actually need to ask the person to forgive you. This puts him in a position of power—something you need to do—and solidifies your commitment to making peace.

PHASE 4: GIVE A PEACE OFFERING

This is not always necessary to do, but by giving a small personalized or customized gift, it shows that you've put advance thought, time, and attention into trying to ensure that you worked things out.

REAL-WORLD, REAL-LIFE EXAMPLE AND SCENARIO

SCENARIO: Jane and John, sister and brother, got into an argument Thanksgiving Day, two weeks earlier—over something silly and nonsensical, but it escalated into a big fight. Since then neither one has talked to the other, and Jane just wants to make peace.

> **JANE:** [phoning her brother] *"John, it's me and I want you to know that I'm sorry. It was my fault entirely. You know how I have always had such respect for you. I just wasn't thinking when I started yelling. Will you please forgive me for being an idiot?"*

JOHN: *"Sure, and it wasn't all your fault. I'm sorry, too."* [If you get a different response, go to Chapter 21.]

You see, John has to know that it wasn't all his sister's fault. But when she takes all the blame, it shows her vulnerability, commitment, and sincerity and forces him to apologize for his role in the argument. But had Jane blamed the situation partly on her brother, she would have risked his getting defensive and escalating the conflict further. This approach disarms the person instantly and melts away the tension, paving the way to easily make peace.

> ✻ FLASH REVIEW ✻
>
> When a conversation turns into a confrontation, you can smooth things over quickly and easily. This four-phase process works by accepting blame, demonstrating a longtime admiration, asking for forgiveness, and giving a peace offering.

CHAPTER 21

WHEN TIME HAS PASSED AND NOBODY'S TALKING, A SIMPLE
YET FAST TECHNIQUE TO BRING BACK THE GOOD OLD DAYS

In this scenario, significant time has passed without interaction or conversation, or you've had nothing but unfriendly encounters. This psychological strategy is for those times when what happened is over and done with, but so much time has passed that you don't even know where to begin and what to say.

STRATEGIC PSYCHOLOGICAL SOLUTION

PHASE 1: APOLOGIZE

Remember, as we said in the previous chapter, you should apologize sincerely and directly and take 100 percent of the blame and responsibility. Now is not the time for a game of "who said what first."

PHASE 2: A MATTER OF RESPECT

Let the person know that your actions were not meant as disrespectful, even though that is how they appeared. Remind him of how much you admire and respect him and apologize specifically for both your actions *and* the lack of respect they showed.

PHASE 3: SHOW YOUR REGRET

Let the person know that you feel bad about your actions and promise him that they will not be repeated.

PHASE 4: DEMONSTRATE PAIN

He should know that you are in pain and suffering from both the guilt of your actions *and* the loss of the friendship and/or relationship. Explain to him what has changed in your life, if anything, since the incident and how it has been difficult for you.

PHASE 5: ASK FOR FORGIVENESS

Directly and specifically ask the person to forgive you.

EMERGENCY PRIMERS

If you think you are going to be met with intense resistance, use any one or all of the following techniques before you start with Phase 1.

A. Tell a Moving Story

Tell a moving story that involves the two of you. This will help to bring her back to a happier time, and the emotions you evoke will help to generate momentum when you use the above five steps.

B. Send a Peace Offering in Advance

Your second option is to send something ahead. The gift creates an unconscious obligation where the other person feels that "the least she can do" is to *listen* to what you have to say.

C. Third-Party Help

If you need to, use the third-party technique in Chapter 27 to get the person to listen to what you have to say, receptively and willingly.

| REAL-WORLD, REAL-LIFE EXAMPLE AND SCENARIO |

SCENARIO: A mother, Geraldine, got into an argument with her daughter Jesse over her daughter's boyfriend. He's no longer in the picture. They each said things that they regret, but for two years they have not spoken.

Again, regardless of who is to blame for what, whoever wants to make peace should admit to bearing full and complete responsibility for what happened. Now is not the time to point fingers. Apologize sincerely and directly and take one hundred percent of the blame. If you take full responsibility, she cannot argue with you. In time, you are welcome to revisit the situation and ask her if she does not feel partly to blame. But do not do it now. Establishing peace is your sole objective at this point.

GERALDINE: [optional emergency primer(s)] *"I want you to know how sorry I am for causing what happened. For the past two years I have done nothing but think about how I could have been so thoughtless and stupid. I was afraid to call because I was so ashamed, even though I wanted very badly for us to have the kind of relationship that we used to. You know I've always respected your decisions as a woman, and even though I didn't always agree I was proud that you stood on your own two feet."*

All Jesse can do is agree as her mother has not given her anything that she can argue with. All Jesse can say is that she, too, bears some of the blame and responsibility for causing the rift between them.

"Do you think you can find it in your heart to forgive me? And before you answer know that I will never, ever speak to you or treat you with such disrespect again."

If you get a response that's not productive, see Chapter 28 and use the emergency techniques.

✳ FLASH REVIEW ✳

When too much time has passed and you want to make peace, this five-phase process will allow you to make things good again. The process includes apologizing, demonstrating respect, showing regret and pain, and asking for forgiveness.

SECTION VI

You Can Be the Great Peacemaker: End Any Estrangement, Conflict, or Feud: When Nobody's Talking—Whether It's Been Twenty Minutes or Twenty Years—Put the Past in the Past and Bring People Together

You *can be the peacemaker and make things good again! Any situation where there is an ongoing squabble or feud and you want to intervene and bring peace, now you can. In any relationship or situation—professional or personal—you can make peace between those who think they don't even want to make it.*

You can even bring people closer together who have grown apart or who simply don't get along very well. Settle feuds and conflicts between any two people, over anything. Repair almost any damaged relationship no matter how bad it's gotten and no matter what was said and done.

If you are one of the parties involved, it might be best to gain the cooperation of a "go-between." Some situations are best resolved with the help of a neutral third party, so gauge the circumstance to see if this isn't one of those times.

Remember, relationships are built on trust, honesty, and respect, so make sure your motivations are good and the benefits to all parties are clear. Please see "A Note to Readers" (page xv) for further clarification of this necessity.

CHAPTER 22

In Any Situation, Personal or Professional, Bring People Closer Together Who Have Either Grown Apart or Who Just Don't Get Along Very Well

Are you having a problem getting people to work well together? Or would you like to improve the relationship between others? Not to worry. With these techniques you can get any group of two or more people to work together in a friendly and cooperative manner.

It doesn't much matter if any one person is at fault, because the one who is responsible clearly doesn't see it this way. We can assume there was a difference of opinion over who did what to whom and who is to blame for what. Or it may be just a general lack of respect for one another manifesting itself in conversations filled with sarcastic remarks and an underlying air of hostility, competition, or jealousy.

AN OLDIE BUT A GOODIE
The Bible tell us that tens of thousands of people attended the funeral of Aaron, Moses's brother—many more than those who attended Moses' funeral. The reason is that whenever there was a squabble between a couple, they would come to Aaron for help. He in turn went to each of the persons involved, separately and privately, and said simply that the other is hurting and in great pain over the fallout. The people who attended his funeral included all of the children of these couples, who if not for him might never have been born.

STRATEGIC PSYCHOLOGICAL SOLUTION

Your overall objective is to give information about each party to the other—information that will change how each person sees the other and consequently interacts and treats the other.

PHASE 1: REESTABLISH RESPECT

Let each person know that the other really respects the way he does a particular thing, or how the other admires something that he stands for or supports. In almost every situation, the reason one person treats the other with a lack of respect is simply that he doesn't feel that he gets respect from the other person.

AND/OR

PHASE 2: DEMONSTRATE CONSEQUENCES

Let each one know that while the other didn't say anything to you outright, you know that each cares a great deal about what the other thinks of him and he might want to *lighten up a bit.* Maybe give some nice words of encouragement, as you know that they will go a long way and make her feel good.

AND/OR

PHASE 3: HUMANIZE

It's easier to do harm to those we do not see as real people, and to those we do not see physically. In war, to drop a bomb on a city can carry less psychological trauma for a pilot than for a soldier to shoot a man at point-blank range. It's good to let the other *know things*—as long as it doesn't violate one's trust and confidence in the other. When we learn that someone was a war veteran, or had a tragedy when young, or is suffering from an illness, we can't help but be more compassionate and empathetic regardless of what we think of him.

You can "mix and match" the above using whatever is most appropriate to the situation. (We'll take an example of each soon.) As long as each person is told *one* of the above, you have probably already greatly decreased any hostility. In most cases one of the people is really causing most of the friction, so you would want to target your technique mostly on him.

CREATE AN OUTSIDE FOCUS

Numerous studies conclude that division among people dissolves when there is an opposing outside threat. Civil war, intersocietal conflicts, and internal unrest often cease when a common outside enemy comes onto the scene. Conversely, individuals more often will turn their attention and hostility to one another when no outside forces are present. The fastest way to instill cooperation between two people is to (a) create an external focus and/or (b) simply set your group against another group in some form of competition.

REAL-WORLD, REAL-LIFE EXAMPLE AND SCENARIO

SCENARIO: A school principal has two teachers who don't get along well. He's not sure what caused the problem, and he doesn't believe he'd get a straight answer if he asked. He simply wants to get them to become more friendly and work together better. (Teacher 1 is the cause of most of the friction.)

PRINCIPAL TO TEACHER 1

> **PRINCIPAL:** *"I've got to tell you, I know that you and Teacher 2 don't always see eye-to-eye on things, but I think some of the remarks you make really upset her."*

TEACHER 1: *"Really? I didn't say anything that rude. Maybe she's just sensitive."*

PRINCIPAL: *"I know, but I happen to know that she has a great deal of respect for you, and the comments sting a bit when they come from someone she really just wants to impress."*

TEACHER 1: *"Oh, okay. I never realized."*

PRINCIPAL: *"I know. So any words of encouragement are going to mean an awful lot to her. Besides, she's been through a lot with her son, who's been in and out of the hospital for the past few years."*

PRINCIPAL TO TEACHER 2

PRINCIPAL: *"You know, I was speaking with Teacher 1 about the upcoming parent conference and she suggested that I ask you for your thoughts."*

[He explains what's going on and then adds] *"I know that you and Teacher 1 have had your moments, but she thinks you're an excellent teacher."*

IT'S NOT SUCH A BIG DEAL

What about those times when the conflict isn't so great but the two people involved just seem to either resent, or are easily annoyed with, each other. Here you have a situation where it is completely about respect, as there are no real issues to deal with. You can make peace very easily and effectively by going to each person and telling him how much the other person really respects the way he does or did something. You will find almost every single time that each person—who now feels respected by the other—begins to act with significant kindness and respect for the other.

✳ FLASH REVIEW ✳

To improve relations between any two people, you only need to demonstrate that each party respects the other and/or is pained by the other person's negative comments or actions. This, coupled with humanizing each to the other, will easily pave the way for better relations.

CHAPTER 23

In these situations the catalyst is gone. Either what caused the rift was
something minor that was blown out of proportion or what once was an
issue is no longer relevant. What's left are just hurt feelings and hurt
people. Nobody's talking and you want to change all that. Here's how
it's done.

Two classes: **Class A:** Current or recent rift
                  Class B: It has evolved into a long-term drift

Class A: Current or Recent Rift

There are situations when just a short time has passed. It's hard to say,
in terms of hours or days, what exactly a short time is, as it really depends on the situation and the usual level of interaction. But we can
say that it usually falls into the short-time category if there has been no
communication or contact, where there should be, for more than one
week and/or two points in time where there would have been normal
interaction.

Class B: Long-Term Drift

Time has passed and the catalyst is old. What caused the rift is of little
importance, and the loss of contact has either frozen or damaged the

relationship. The problem is no longer the issues but rather the passage of time. And with no one "doing anything," the bond that was once shared has now all but dissipated.

STRATEGIC PSYCHOLOGICAL SOLUTION

CLASS A: CURRENT OR RECENT RIFT

Research in this area shows that a quick jump-start is the best way to get things back on track. This is accomplished by using one or a combination of the following techniques. You can pick and choose what makes the most sense given the situation, including how much leverage you have, the ages of those involved, and the context.

Option 1: Put them in a situation that is humorous. Psychologically speaking, when we are in a situation that we don't take seriously, these feelings get transferred where *we don't take ourselves*—within this context—*so seriously.* And when it comes to the ego, if you can make light of the *situation,* you help loosen the grip of self-righteousness.

Option 2: Give them a shot of reality. Have them work together in a soup kitchen or hospital. Or set it up where they visit someone who is sick, injured, or in deep poverty. Even something like watching a short film or tape on a natural disaster or emergency-room scene can be effective. Anything that makes them realize what is *important* and what is not. This helps to realign their unconscious priorities and see what really matters. After this, the conflict is put into the proper perspective and shakes out as something that is silly and unnecessary.

Option 3: Demonstrate to each person how the other respects him and is suffering because of the lack of communication. Couple this with an objective review of the situation and a willingness on each person's part to move past the conflict.

Option 4: Have them work together toward a common goal. Studies as well as life experience show us that any time people work together on a common objective, it creates an "us against the world" mentality. So create a situation where they are teamed up and their mutual co-operation will dictate their success. Interestingly enough, whether or not they succeed or fail does not matter as long as each person believes that the other did his best and pulled his own weight. Win or lose, it still creates a bond.

REAL-WORLD, REAL-LIFE EXAMPLE AND SCENARIO

CLASS A

SCENARIO: A few days ago, two police officers got into an argument over a case. It was originally a misunderstanding, but words were exchanged and now the two don't speak except for passing sarcastic remarks. The lieutenant in charge wants the two officers to reconcile.

Application of Option 1: He handcuffs them together and puts them in a room by themselves and they're instructed that they can only come out when they say five nice things about each other. (I know what you're thinking, but trust me, it works. Especially if other people are around to make it more "festive.")

Application of Option 2: He has them watch a video of an emergency-room victim, or has them visit with the widow of a former policeman.

Application of Option 3: The lieutenant relates to each one, privately, how the other regrets that the two of them are no longer friendly. He lets each one know that the other has great respect for him.

Application of Option 4: He puts them together on a case, interview, or interrogation. Or he puts them in charge of the office New Year's party or orphan fund drive.

> If you do not meet with the success you want, go to Chapter 28, "In Case of Emergency."

✳ FLASH REVIEW ✳

When something minor gets blown out of proportion, get people talking again with one of four psychological options. The techniques allow you to quickly put out the fire before it spreads and does any real damage.

CLASS B: LONG-TERM DRIFT

Because some time has passed, we don't have the luxury of trying a sampling of tactics until we hit one that works. Here we have to be more precise in our strategy.

PHASE 1: REESTABLISH GOOD FEELINGS

Ideally, you want to reestablish the relationship in the thoughts of each person, meaning that you bring each one back into the other person's life—first in their mind. Since some time has passed, the relationship may not be taking center stage in their lives. And if they are not thinking about each other, they don't feel as if they are missing anything. Using one or more of the following tactics will help to get the mental ball rolling.

- To each person, tell a humorous or touching story about the two of them, from the "good old days."
- Let each person know that the other was asking or always asks how the other is doing and is concerned when things are not going well.
- Reestablish mutual respect by letting each one know that the other speaks well of him and often praises his actions, lifestyle, choices, and so on.

PHASE 2: TRY FOR A FAST SOLUTION

Now you gauge the situation to see if you can end this fast. To one of the people, say the following:

"Mitch is very sorry for what happened and regrets that the two of you are not speaking. I know that if you made the first move and called, he would be eager to hear from you. I know he's sorry for how things unfolded. After so much time, he feels so bad and can't bring himself to make the first move."

Next:

- If he agrees, then skip to Phase 7 and continue from there. If he does not, then go to the other person with the same technique. If the other person agrees, then continue to Phase 7. If neither one agrees, then read on.

PHASE 3: ONE MORE TRY

Before you abandon this option, if neither will commit to calling, see how either feels about writing a letter or having *you* call with a message from him. Anything that begins to build momentum is positive and productive. If you still have no success at this point, then continue. If one agrees, then proceed to Phase 6.

PHASE 4: THE CROWBAR

You want to see if either person is simply putting up a strong front. This technique will help you to decide whether the person is or isn't really interested in reestablishing the relationship.

I first wrote about this technique in *Get Anyone to Do Anything* and found its application in situations like this to be highly effective. If you want to know whether or not those involved will ever make peace and which one will be likely to yield first, this technique will give you that answer in about five minutes. Note: All techniques, this and the ones throughout the chapter, are used separately, on each person, and in private.

Tell the person that she has to agree to doing what you ask, but *only* if you can achieve some highly difficult and amazing task. For instance, you would ask her to think of a number from one to one hundred and if you can guess what it is then she will agree to hearing you out and/or agreeing to make peace. She will probably agree, because she believes that there is little chance that you can guess right. If she *does not* agree to these terms, then it is likely that she is adamant about her stance. In doing this you accomplish several things—most notably being able to determine who is going to be the one who will need a harder sell and who is more likely to consider mending fences. If both readily agree, then you know you've got an easier job.

The psychological strategy here is not in being right, although if you are that's great. Rather, it's in *her agreeing to take the chance.* Again, if at this point she absolutely refuses, then you know what you're up against. But if she does agree, then you've managed to adjust her belief system slightly—and this is all you need. You take her from a *no* to a *maybe.* Now she will have to alter her belief system to allow the possibility—though remote—for a reunion to happen. In order to reduce dissonance, she unconsciously adjusts her thinking and will now become more open. Only someone who in the back of her mind is willing to make peace would take part in this test. So some part of her, to some degree, is willing. Now you know that you're not faced with an impossible task. And you see that you've reshaped her self-concept to included the definition of someone who is open and interested. This is precisely the image you want her to hold of herself, since your request falls outside of her usual comfort zone.

Next:

- If one or both persons want nothing to do with the other, then go to the techniques in Chapter 28, "In Case of Emergency."
- If both people play along, then go to the next technique.

PHASE 5: GATHERING AMMUNITION AND ICEBREAKERS

Now you know that you're dealing with willing participants, so you need to gather firepower that you can use. If the two people keep saying why they are mad and why they hate the other and want nothing to do with him, then their thoughts are locked into an unproductive cycle. To change this, ask a series of questions that move them into the frame of making peace. Ask questions such as:

- "What would you have done differently?"
- "Do you regret how things have turned out?"
- "If you could erase that day, would you?"
- "What did you enjoy from the relationship?"
- "Do you remember any of the good times?"

What these questions do is give you ammunition for two objectives. One is when *you* go to each person and the second is when *they both meet*. When you go to each person and say that the other said, "He wishes he could erase that day," or "He regrets how things have turned out," you have room to create a resolution.

Second, when you go to the next stage of planning the outcome, you want to be sure that each person is armed with something to say to break the ice. Ask each person, *What would you have to hear from the other to begin to talk again?* The answers to these questions give you such icebreakers such as "I'm sorry how things unfolded," or "I never should have provoked you." This gives you the opportunity to see where the answer to this question blends in with the answers to each of the above questions. "I shouldn't have said what I did" can be easily translated into an apology if one is listening for it.

Phase 6: What Will It Take?

Now that they are in the right mental mode, ask: "What would you have to hear from the other person to begin to talk again?" Or "What would he have to do to begin to make things right?"

Next:

- If neither respond with anything reasonable, go to Chapter 28, "In Case of Emergency."
- If you get a reasonable response from one or both, then proceed

to the next phase. Note: It's important to emphasize to each person that the other is excited and grateful to be able to put this behind him. Knowing that the other person is eager to reconcile helps both people focus on the relationship and not on the conflict.

PHASE 7: PLAN THE OUTCOME

When you get them to agree to talk, make sure you plan it out. You take care of all the details. Don't say, "Just meet somewhere and talk it out." *You arrange everything* and, most important, agree with each person what he will say to the other when they *first meet.* Ideally, each person should be readied with the following:

A. Whether it's an apology of some sort or the expression of a willingness to listen or an expression of regret, you need to have the icebreakers ready to go or you risk an uncomfortable conversation marred with standoffish behavior. Take the answers you get from Phase 5 to arm each person with something positive to say.

AND/OR

B. If you can't think of icebreakers that you like or can use, remember that your overall objective is to get each person to see the situation from the other's point of view. Therefore, let each person know why the other did what he did and have that person reiterate it when they meet. For instance, "I know that you got so upset with me because you had my best interest at heart." *This validates each person's actions!*

These two ideas are gentle ways of saying and showing that each person is interested in moving past this conflict and reestablishing a trusting relationship.

PHASE 8: SOLIDIFY AFTER THE FACT

Once there is a reconciliation, sometimes *buyer's remorse* sets in. This is a term used in sales when the buyer has second thoughts about his purchase. The same thing could easily happen here, where one person thinks, "Did I make a fool of myself?" or "Did he take me seriously?" etc. Therefore, it is up to you to seal the process by letting each person know—individually, of course—that the other person feels great about what has taken place and how the renewed friendship and/or relationship has made him happy and grateful.

REAL-WORLD, REAL-LIFE EXAMPLE AND SCENARIO

SCENARIO: Two mothers-in-law got into an argument over the wedding of their children and have not spoken for three years. The children—son and daughter—want them to reconcile.

CHILD TO EACH MOTHER

"I was speaking to Cynthia and she reminded me of the story of when you two went shopping for the wedding dress and got locked in the dressing room. You know, whenever I speak to her, she's always asking about you. And when you were sick that time, she must have called a half-dozen times to check on how you were."

[Quick settle] *"She feels just awful that the two of you are not speaking, and for what happened. I know that if you called, she would love to hear from you. After so much time, she feels so bad and is too embarrassed to call."*

[Second try] *"If you'll let me, I'll call her and set it up. Why don't we all go to lunch, and put this nonsense behind us. I know she'd like that."*

The children proceed to Phase 4 to gather icebreakers for when the mothers meet. They ask questions such as, *"Let me ask you this: Do you have any regrets how things turned out?"* Or *"What would you have done differently?"*

The children arrange for everyone to meet, arming each person with something to say. For instance, Mother 1 would be asked to say that she missed the relationship, and Mother 2 would be told that it would be good for her to say that she is sorry for how things got out of hand.

Then the children solidify the reunion afterward by letting each mother know that the other really enjoyed being on good terms again and is grateful for the reunion.

If you do not meet with the success you want, go to Chapter 28, "In Case of Emergency."

* FLASH REVIEW *

Most rifts of this type can be resolved quickly by using an eight-phase strategy that allows everyone involved to move past the conflict. This is accomplished by focusing on the relationship itself, shifting the parties perspective, and realigning their focus.

CHAPTER 24

The Estranged Relationship: "It's Nothing You Did. I Just Don't Like You and What You Stand For": Resolving Conflicts over Beliefs, Values, and Lifestyle

The relationship that is in difficulty because of a clash of beliefs or values usually involves a cause that has an acronym for its name—from NRA to GLADD to PETA. What one person espouses doesn't jibe with the other's sense of what is *right*.

But this chapter raises a larger question. At what point do you decide that someone else's beliefs or lifestyle are *too* antithetical to what you believe? So much so that you do not want this person in your life? There are times when it would be in everyone's best interest not to have contact. Just because you can resolve an estrangement doesn't always mean that you should.

These techniques are for situations where one person objects to the other. Whether it's over beliefs, lifestyle, attitude, values, or political affiliation, nothing has changed except that time has passed. They never saw eye to eye over this issue and still don't. And it's become your own little Middle East crisis.

> If you are one of the two people involved, then find a third party to engage these techniques for you. In some cases conflicts are best resolved with the help of a neutral party, and this is certainly one of those times.

STRATEGIC PSYCHOLOGICAL SOLUTION

Now we've seen the impact that respect has on a relationship. And here it is *doubly compounded.* The reason is this: If you object to a person's *beliefs, values,* or *lifestyle,* you not only don't respect his ideas but essentially don't have "respect" for *him,* since they are intertwined with *who he is.*

One says, "How can I have any respect for someone who is . . . pro-life . . . a Republican . . . gay?" and so on. And the other says, "How can I have a relationship with someone who won't respect my choices?" Common sense will tell you that these two will not get along. Therefore we put our focus on reshaping how each person *sees* the other, and easily resolve what appears to be an intricate and unresolvable estrangement.

GET OUT OF MY FACE!

Make sure that whoever's behavior or values are disliked, this person does not flaunt it. He would choose to *not* listen to this advice for two reasons: Either he doesn't respect the other person and so doesn't care about further irritating him, or he doesn't believe in his cause enough himself so he needs to publicly declare his beliefs in order to reinforce his own self-doubt.

Where do you begin?

This is a fantastic strategy that can melt even the most hardened hearts and the most stubborn minds.

PHASE 1: REFOCUS PERCEPTION

This is done through giving the person who objects to the other the opportunity to see that this person is a *good person,* in order to *dilute* his objection.

For instance, if John lacks respect for Mary because she's pro-choice and he's a strong pro-life proponent, it would be difficult for them to have a relationship or friendship of any sort. But if Mary donates a kidney to a relative, works with handicapped children, and reads to the blind in her spare time, his perception of her *might* change. *But* if John has a favorite uncle who is blind, and John is the recipient of a transplanted kidney himself, and has a handicapped son, *he can't help but respect Mary for what she does.*

Obviously, this is an extreme example, but we can see through this illustration that John is forced to reconcile his feelings about Mary. Can he still hate her? Psychological research shows overwhelmingly that he cannot. He still will not respect her views and he will still maintain that she's wrong, but unless he has a split personality, he is psychologically forced, first unconsciously then consciously, to reshape his thoughts to be more positive toward her.

Respect lies in identifying with the virtues of another person. To respect and like someone, you need only identify with that person's positive traits. Consequently, when you choose to dislike someone, you identify him with his faults. The reasons you give are negative qualities: He is arrogant, annoying, and cheap. When you think of someone you like, you identify with his good qualities: He is kind, generous, and open-minded.

Does this mean that he has no bad traits? Of course not—it's just what you *choose* to focus on. If you shift your focus, you can look at anyone in an entirely new way. If you can't find anything in common, then use any admirable qualities, values, or beliefs that they share, and amplify them to this person.

PHASE 2: ENGAGE THE LAWS OF GUILT-REDUCTION AND COGNITIVE DISSONANCE

Once the initial conflict develops, it spirals downward to the point where lack of respect for the other increases on both sides. This gives each person ammunition for disliking the other, and for grounding their disapproval (or hatred) in more permanent reasons. Disliking someone because of his lifestyle or values does not usually give a person the psychological motivation to *continue* to dislike him. (In general maybe, but not once a relationship has existed.)

But if somebody treats us poorly, then we have a clear-cut, apparent, and obvious reason for disliking him. And *this* is why these types of estrangements are often so tricky to resolve. It's not so much the initial disdain that one or both hold, but rather the spiral that forces the relationship to further deteriorate until it dissipates. If you do not give him a *substantial* reason to dislike you, then his hostility will often dissolve. Substantial is defined as focused, intentional disrespect. Understand that this person may never come to accept your views, but this does not mean that he will not accept *you*, as long as you don't give him a reason to maintain his initial conclusion that you are a bad person because you hold an opposing view. This technique separates in his mind the reason from the behavior or belief. Proof of this is that many people have a friendship or relationship with someone they disagree vehemently with, but they are able to separate this attribute from the person himself.

You want to make it so his negative attitude toward you does not stick and form into a belief about you as a person. Even if much time has passed, you can still reverse the slide. This is done by showing complete respect for him *in spite of* his comments to you and his treatment of you. This validates him while invalidating his attitude toward you.

This method engages *two* very powerful psychological principles. The first is called cognitive dissonance. If you're treating a person well in spite of how badly he's treating you, then he has to reconcile why it is he's being rude and intolerant to somebody who is kind and respectful to him. In order to justify and resolve this contradiction, the person naturally eliminates one of the beliefs. He needs to unconsciously resolve the contradiction—if you're such a bad person, why are you so kind and good to him? *One* of his beliefs will have to budge. Research tells us that he will be forced to conclude that you must be a good person who holds a wrong belief instead of a bad person whom he would likely want nothing to do with.

Second, this method also engages what is called guilt reduction. Studies show us that human beings will do almost anything to eliminate feelings of guilt. As we know in our own life, guilt can be very damaging and the cause of many self-destructive behaviors. When you're treating him kindly and he's treating you poorly, he will at some level, to some degree, feel guilty. If you were rude to him and he disliked you, then that's easy enough to justify. But now, in order to reconcile this guilt, he changes his behavior to one that is *more tolerant and understanding.* As soon as the guilt gets too much, as a matter of self-preservation he will go the course of least resistance. In effect, the kinder you are, the greater the pressure.

This of course does not mean that anyone should be a verbal punching bag, but you will find in a very short time that his behavior begins to realign itself to be more accepting. Note: If there is no direct contact, then this change of attitude may be conveyed through letters, tapes, mutual friends, and relatives.

PHASE 3: RESHAPE THE SITUATION

Next is to reshape the situation to be *temporary, isolated,* and *insignificant.* How we deal with new information depends on how it is internalized. When a person becomes upset about an event in her life, it's often because of three mental beliefs: (1) she feels that the situation is *permanent;* (2) she feels that it is *critical,* meaning that it's more significant than it really is; and (3) she feels that it is *all-consuming,* that it will invade and pervade other areas of her life.

When any or all of these beliefs are present and elevated, it will dramatically increase her anger and resentment. Conversely, if she thinks of the person's beliefs or values as *temporary, isolated,* and *insignificant,* it doesn't concern her as much.

WHY?

Why are we sometimes bothered or angered by beliefs or values different from ours? Simple. We live our life a certain way, and when someone comes along and believes differently from the way we do, we either (a) become threatened that we may be wrong or (b) feel anger that their values will have a negative impact on people and things that we care about. There are other mitigating causes of inner hostility, such as guilt, resentment, shame, and embarrassment. But at its root hostility comes from seeing that someone is doing something that goes against the way we feel it should be. Our sense of right and wrong is being challenged, and this can make us fearful and cause us to lash out. While it is, of course, okay to disagree and not want a relationship with someone who you believe violates what is right, actual anger at someone for holding an opposing view is not healthy or productive.

Take any situation—for instance, someone being told that she has a heart condition. The first question she asks is, "How will it affect my life? What can't I do? What do I have to do? Will I have it forever or is it a short-term condition?"

By artificially inflating these factors (*temporary, isolated,* and *insignificant*), you can instantly alter someone's attitude toward a situation. While the circumstances will dictate how this method can best be used, if you can address at least one of these, you will be effective in diminishing an unpleasant reaction. Also, these factors should be kept in mind when initially "breaking" the news.

PHASE 4: GENERATE INTERNAL CONSISTENCY: PEOPLE IN MOTION TEND TO STAY IN MOTION

Get your way by invoking the powerful psychological law of *internal consistency*. Studies in human behavior show us that you can change a person's thoughts by changing how he sees himself. The psychological technique allows you to change a person's self-concept so that it is flexible and giving: the exact frame of mind that you want him in.

What is most fascinating is that you can reshape a person's self-concept in under a minute. How can you do this so quickly? Well, in actuality what you are doing is changing how that person sees himself *in relation to you* only. Which is fine here, since that is what you want. But this would not be so effective to change how the person sees herself in general.

This is done with a simple, well-orchestrated phrase. And in this case we know how we want the person to see himself—as someone who is flexible and open-minded. So you would say, at a time when things are fine, something such as, "I've always admired the way you aren't afraid to change your mind." Or "You really know that communication is what a relationship is all about. I very much respect that." Or "You never lose sight of what is really important in a relationship. I admire that."

These phrases make the person feel compelled to follow through, because you involve the ego and create a sense of desired consistency. People have an inherent need to perform in a matter consistent with how they see themselves and with how they think others perceive them.

I remember once when I was explaining this idea to a colleague I decided to have some fun. When he came to my office and sat down, I offered him some fruit. He hesitated for a moment and then gave an unsure, "No, thanks." I took a nice ripe apple and I saw that he was about to change his mind. That's when I said, "You know what I like about you? You're not wishy-washy. You make a decision and you stick to it. You're a man who knows what he wants." After I said that, it became very hard for him to ask for the fruit—as he later acknowledged—because it would shatter my image of him. Of course, I only let this go on for a minute before clueing him in, and then watched him eagerly devour a peach.

Another way to apply this psychology is by incorporating *themes*, such as friendship, family, partnership, commitment to work, a sense of decency—all qualities that most people aspire to identify with. A phrase like "Isn't it amazing how some people don't know the definition of the word 'family'? is so powerful. With this one statement, you bring someone's value system—what is important to her—into the situation. Now the present situation becomes not an isolated instance but something that actually defines your friendship or relationship. She's risking more than just being confrontational or stubborn, she's risking having to reevaluate what kind of person she is.

PHASE 5: PLAN THE OUTCOME

If you are acting as a third party, don't say, "Just meet somewhere and talk it out." *You arrange everything,* and most important, agree with each person what he will say to the other when they *first meet.*

The focus should be twofold. First, let the person know (the one who objects to the other) that he will be in complete control of the situation and what happens. And second, find for them *common ground* to speak about that is *unrelated* to the objectionable trait or belief or lifestyle. It's okay for people to agree to disagree. What they don't share does not have to be the focal point of the conversation or of the relationship. Have them talk about other things of common interest and appreciation.

SPECIAL TACTIC

If there is some contact, just keep doing the techniques and you'll be on your way. If there is no contact, then the third party needs to get the two of them talking—in some cases, by any means necessary. As they don't have a relationship to speak of, it will be tough to cause any damage. Giving one party the opportunity to "make his case" as to why she's wrong may present the opportunity for the two of them to talk. Even though the discussion is bound to be tumultuous, you've begun to open the lines of communication. *"I think you spoke to her, and even if you don't want to reconcile, I think that now she'd be more receptive to hearing why you think it's wrong."*

This strategy assumes a willingness on the part of the other person to do whatever it takes to make peace. If this is not the case, then go to Chapter 28, "In Case of Emergency."

Also, if you can't get one person to listen to the other, see Chapter 27 for specific techniques on how to do this.

REAL-WORLD, REAL-LIFE EXAMPLE AND SCENARIO

SCENARIO: A woman is trying to make peace between her husband and their estranged daughter, a lesbian. She has been "disowned" by her father because of her sexual preference. Father and daughter have drifted apart over the last few years.

Conversation A: The mother/wife (Fran) speaks to her husband, Bill

> *"You know, she has been giving a lot of time to the veterans' hospital because she knows how important and helpful they were to you in your recovery. And she has your love of gardening."*

If there is contact between the two, then the daughter is treating her father with the utmost respect and deference. This will engage the cognitive dissonance and guilt-reduction theories. If there is no contact, then once it is established, the daughter puts these psychological laws into action. In the meantime, she attempts through third-party contacts, letters, and tapes to convey this. This is very powerful and is continued until no longer necessary.

> *"She may just be going through a phase—she's said as much. She still does the same old things she's always done. She's the same daughter. And she needs your guidance most of all now."*

I know you may be thinking that it is wrong to play down a person's sexual preference in this way. But the larger objective must be kept in mind. You can't simply say that if he doesn't love her for who she is, then he shouldn't be in her life. We all need time to adjust and grow, and the best way to do that is to keep strands of the relationship alive until the person comes around. And this will give you the best chance to do that.

Conversation B: The mother/wife (Fran) speaks to her daughter Jane

> *"I know you are not the kind of person to give up on anyone. In fact, that's one of the things I've always admired so much about you."*

What if you hear something such as, *"If he won't accept me for who I am, then I don't want him in my life."* Then you will probably need to go to Chapter 28, "In Case of an Emergency."

The key here is to emphasize the daughter's need to be flexible and understanding. She must know that the truth meted out in small bits is usually better digested then a main course of hard-to-swallow reality. If she wants a relationship, this will need to be conveyed to her. She needs to be reminded that

- The larger picture must be kept in mind.
- Having a relationship with someone who is stubborn and closed-minded or even bigoted may be better than no relationship at all.
- He still loves her but just doesn't understand.
- Tomorrow is guaranteed to no one, and now may be her only chance to try.

Additionally, the same techniques Fran uses on her husband can be used with her daughter.

YOU CAN ALWAYS FIND SOMETHING TO DISAGREE OVER

The fact is that many people have friends and relationships with those who have fundamentally different beliefs. The secret is no secret, but don't bring it up. This is often a perfectly fine, healthy alternative. It's okay to agree to disagree. Not every issue needs a thorough, complete, and intensive investigation. If you want to find something to argue about, you will have no shortage of topics. Smart people find things they can agree on, and respect or at least tolerate the other's views and/or behaviors.

If you do not meet with the success you want, go to Chapter 28, "In Case of Emergency."

✳ FLASH REVIEW ✳

Almost every conflict of this type can be dissolved by a process that includes (1) getting the person to refocus how he sees the other person, (2) engage the psychological principles of cognitive dissonance and the theory of guilt reduction, and (3) confine the objectionable value or belief by isolating it, making it temporary and noncritical.

CHAPTER 25

FACTS AND FAIRNESS: WHAT CREATED THE RIFT IS *STILL*
RELEVANT: WHEN IT'S EVERYBODY FOR HIMSELF, LEARN
THE KEYS TO SETTLING ANY DEADLOCK IN A MEDIATION,
ARBITRATION, OR NEGOTIATION

The catalyst of this conflict is relevant. Nothing has changed except
that time has passed. These psychological techniques are for settling
conflicts when it's everybody for himself.

There are many books specifically on the subject of conflict resolution. Volumes have been written on subjects ranging from negotiating
union contracts to insights into the Middle East peace process. Some
of the ideas are excellent, while other well-intentioned books offer
such handy hints as "Conflicts are your tummy's way of saying that
something isn't right." And are drizzled with such commonsense gems
as "Conflicts are created when people see things differently." These
nuggets of gold beg the obvious question of, Now what?

We are not going to launch into a discussion of the different mathe-
matical equations for equitable distribution, nor will we repeat patently
obvious advice. Rather, we are going to cut to the chase and explain
clearly and concisely how you can *maximize your advantage* to help
settle any dispute or claim—whether you are directly involved or involved as a third party—by understanding *the fundamental psychology
at play.*

There are *universal psychological principles* that can be overlaid
onto any situation. Understand, it doesn't matter whether you're di-
viding up assets in a divorce, arguing over an estate, or negotiating a
contract, arbitration, or mediation. Everybody just wants his fair
share.

Hmmm. And so we begin to get to the true essence of these types of conflict. What does this mean, *fair share*? What is *right* is often different from what is *fair*, and *equality* may have nothing to do with *sameness*.

For example, if you had two people who wanted to divide up a pizza and a salad, what would be an equal distribution? Clearly to give each person half of each. But what if one party is lactose-intolerant? Then while it would be an *equal* distribution, it would not be *right*. We can see that the idea of fairness bends depending upon individual needs and desires.

STRATEGIC PSYCHOLOGICAL SOLUTION

Whether it's a negotiation, arbitration, or mediation, research in this area shows us some fascinating insights into how best to gain the edge in any situation. Essentially, it suggests that four quite powerful laws of human nature are always at work and responsible for tilting the conflict to either resolution or escalation.

This is because *what is fair bends*. That is to say, fairness is *never* objective. Your job is to bend it so that from each person's perspective, it feels as if he is getting what is *fair*. This is done by adjusting the laws as explained below. Change these factors and you change the dynamics of any conflict.

LAW 1: THE LAW OF SCARCITY

Would you like a free diamond ring? Or maybe you would rather have an aluminum can? Which do you want *more*, and *why*? Of course the ring, as it's perceived as more valuable because of the degree of availability in relation to demand. It is human nature to want what is rare, to want what we cannot have, and to want more of what we have to work for. So how do you apply the law of scarcity?

Research shows it is applied by reducing the other side's expectations and options—or both sides if you are a mediator. Options give leverage. And if each side believes that he can get a better deal *by go-*

ing elsewhere or *waiting*, you will not resolve the dispute. Only when they understand that they will lose more if they delay can you expect cooperation.

The fact is that if each party believes that the offer will always be on the table and that to maximize his side he needs only to wait or that he won't lose anything by waiting, he will not seek to resolve the situation.

Everything has deadlines or expiration dates. From coupons to us (meaning we don't live forever), deadlines force action. It is human nature to often wait and procrastinate until conditions become more favorable or until we are in a better mood before we seek to take action. It's important to give a clear-cut deadline and let the person know that the action must be taken *now*, because he won't have a chance to later. This also incorporates another psychological principle: that we don't like our freedom to be restricted. By letting him know that he may not get the opportunity to act in the future, you cause him to perceive what he has or can get now as more valuable, and he will move to preserve it.

LAW 2: THE LAW OF CONTRAST AND COMPARISON

Is $300 a fair price for a watch? It's hard to say. But if you told me that it used to sell for $1,600, I would assume that $300 is fair. The degree to which we are *satisfied* with what we get depends mostly on this law.

> Q In what situation can you give someone the moon and they would still not be satisfied?
> A If there are three moons and the other guy just got two of them. "How come he gets two moons? That's not fair!"

Let's see how to use this law to your advantage *and* how to keep it from harming you. It is best to understate the value of a commodity to each side. If each side feels that he is being "ripped off," the situation will not be resolved anytime soon. From land deals to union contracts to severance packages. It all comes down to "What am I getting and what will it do for me?" versus "What are they getting and what will it do for them?"

LAW 3: THE LAW OF RECIPROCITY

There's a rule of persuasion called *reciprocation* that basically says, When someone does us a favor we often feel the need to reciprocate. Have you ever been in a situation where someone does something for you and you feel uncomfortable unless you can pay him back in some way? We know we don't *have* to, but we are often uneasy until we can reciprocate.

When someone gives us something, we feel as if we have to repay the debt. Why? Because it creates a sense of dependency. And as we mentioned in the beginning of the book, in order to feel good about themselves human beings *cannot be dependent.* We need to have a sense of independence to have self-respect. So how is this law applied?

Any side that *gives in* to the other creates a sense of dependency in the other side. In order to regain a sense of independence, the other side feels that it's okay to reciprocate, because he would no longer be the only one who is giving in—which would make him feel weak. Therefore, any concession that one side makes pulls the other—unconsciously—closer to the middle. If both sides walk in with a position that they cannot budge from, you will not have enacted this psychological law of reciprocity and will not be likely to gain cooperation.

LAW 4: THE LAW OF RATIONAL RESPONSE

The final factor has to do with emotions. That is, when the parties respond with emotion, rather than rationally, we are unlikely to assume that the best mind-set is being established. No strategy can be effective as long as the persons are not responding with reason. If someone is emotionally charged, particularly with anger, the normal rules go right out the window.

Therefore careful attention has to be paid to making sure that there is no added animosity from and to each side. This is best achieved by making sure that each party treats the other with *respect* and *courtesy* at all times. Shouting, slanderous statements, and gestures of hostility will cause the conflict to stall time and again. Much research in this area concludes that when anger is reduced, an agreement has a significantly stronger possibility of being reached.

> ### GET SMART
> If you remove the people and the personalities from the equation and look only at the facts, you eliminate up to ninety percent of the obstacles. This much makes sense to us. Why then do we so often insist that the parties meet face-to-face? Unless you are dealing with a family situation whereby you're expecting to produce strong *positive* emotions from both sides, this is not always a good idea. In fact it rarely is. Therefore, meet with each party *separately*, at least initially, to best gauge where you are and what needs to be done in order to effectively engage the four laws of resolution.

REAL-WORLD, REAL-LIFE EXAMPLE AND SCENARIO

There are a multitude of variables in each and every scenario and situation. These techniques can be overlaid onto any system you use.

SCENARIO: You are mediating the severance package between Bill and the company.

You need to make each party aware of the other's options. For instance, the company should know that Bill has legal resources and has influence with a local paper—if, of course, this is true. Bill needs to know that the company will be laying off more people in a short time and that if this case is not resolved now, it will get lost in a sea of others. By emphasizing that no one benefits by delay, you greatly enhance the chances for resolution.

Furthermore, if each party comes in with no room to negotiate, each will be seen as unyielding. Additionally, the law of reciprocity will never be engaged. Therefore, give each side "wiggle room" in order to make concessions and build positive momentum. Bill should be told to come in with a high demand and then make concessions. This engages the law of contrast/comparison as well as the law of reciprocity. And during the negotiations, he should be respectful to all and encouraged not to become emotionally charged. And to be clear, being passionate about your cause is well and good, but once it spills over into hostility, you have begun to harm the process.

Remember, if these laws are not engaged in your favor, resolving the conflict can almost never happen. Look at the Middle East. None of the laws is in play.

If you do not meet with the success you want, go to Chapter 28, "In Case of Emergency."

✳ FLASH REVIEW ✳

Almost every conflict of this type is governed by four laws of psychology that can *bend* the situation. Whether it's a negotiation, arbitration, or mediation, research shows that these four powerful laws of human nature are always at work, and responsible for tilting the conflict to either resolution or escalation.

L P A

LIEBERMAN PROFILE ANALYSIS
WHAT ARE MY ODDS?

LPA is the psychological framework that's used to determine the probable outcome of most situations—whether you gain cooperation or meet with obstinate determination on the part of the other person(s).

A. High esteem/high confidence: This person (or party) feels that he is right and doesn't mind sticking to his guns. *Cooperation is unlikely.*

B. High esteem/low confidence: This produces the *optimum equation,* as the person does not feel strong in his stance yet maintains enough self-esteem to recognize, admit to error, and/or to agree to your request.

C. Low esteem/low confidence: With this makeup, agreement is *undetermined,* as low confidence in his position pushes toward agreement, while low esteem pulls away just when he needs to take—to feed his ego. Giving in or extensive compromise will make him feel weaker.

D. Low esteem/high confidence: This produces *the least possible probability* for cooperation. The person feels strong in his position and will define his self-worth on the outcome, since esteem is low. This psychological dynamic produces the worst combination. This person will be stubborn and unyielding.

The great news is that in *any situation* you find yourself, adjusting these factors to where you increase *esteem* and decrease *confidence* will increase success. The more sure the person is of himself, the more willing he is to give, give in, and see objectively. Additionally, the less confident he feels in his position, the more likely he will be to change his mind, and can do so with ease where esteem is high.

CHAPTER 26

THE FAMILY FEUD OVER $$$: END IT NOW

Money is the single biggest cause of family rifts. It tears at the fabric of our relationships with razorlike teeth. But we can do something to prevent this from happening. I think what's most sad is when people fight over money they don't need. Children go to court to battle it out to see who gets millions of dollars. The winner gets to move the money to an account with his number. Never seen, never touched, never used. Many times, of course, the argument is over money that *is* needed, for necessities, not luxuries, and each person may have a fairly valid claim to it. There are essentially two main areas where money becomes an issue.

TYPE 1: ARGUMENTS OVER SPENDING

This is where family members fight over who spends how much and on what. Every time one person comes home with something new, it's an argument waiting to happen. For example, the wife thinks her husband is a spend-a-holic, and the husband thinks his wife is stingy.

TYPE 2: ALLOCATION OF FUNDS

Here you have a fixed sum and more than one person laying claim to it. Whether it's Uncle Freddy's estate or an argument over who should pay for the broken tractor, money seems to bring out the worst in people.

TYPE 1

The solution is extremely simple. Establish a budget (or call it a *spending strategy,* if the word "budget" offends anyone). This allows the person who is spending the money to feel a sense of independence and control and not that he constantly has to answer to someone. Now, instead of arguing every time he spends a dime on anything, they just have one discussion over the budget, one time. And then they are done arguing about money. (To get the budget that you want, please see Chapter 13.)

But wait a minute! Lots of families have budgets. And if you've lived in an apartment with thin walls, you know that these people *still* argue. Loudly. This is true. Because unless *two rules* are met and abided by, a budget cannot work.

Rule 1: The person giving the money must pass no judgments and make no comments on *how* the money is spent. No looks, no faces, no sarcasm. Nothing.

Rule 2: The person spending the money must be considerate and discreet when it comes to purchasing items that he or she believes will cause the other to be annoyed or upset.

This is why it breaks down. These rules must be put in place for any *spending plans* to work.

REALIGNMENT OF VALUES

It all comes down to values. If you feel that the other "just doesn't get it," then it's because you have a different value system. What you think is important is not what he does. A realignment of values may be a good idea, so that either the one spending the money can see that there are more important things in life that the money can be used for or the one who has it can see that life is too short to keep it stuffed away in a bank and not do anything with it. Doing something such as going to the hospital to visit the sick or going to a funeral puts both in touch with their own mortality, and they can recognize who they really are and what is really important. This will help to strike a balance where they are put in touch with what is important and a happy medium can be struck. Mortality is the great equalizer.

Also, when we are entirely in control of the situation, we tend to feel a greater sense of responsibility. Giving this person complete autonomy over how she spends her money will go a long way toward not only improving the relationship but also avoiding conflicts over money.

STRATEGIC PSYCHOLOGICAL SOLUTION

TYPE 2

These types of conflicts arise over fixed assets, whether it's money itself or something of monetary or sentimental value. From each person's perspective, he is right. "I'm a nice guy and he's being a jerk. It belongs to me."

Here's the story. Money tears at the strands of the relationship. If it is strong, it will not rip. Conflicts over money are like a psychological illness in the relationship. And as with a physical illness, there are two strategies for treating it. Cancer, for instance, is treated by attacking the disease using chemotherapy. Unfortunately, this weakens the person's *overall* immune system. A second method—sometimes, though not often enough, used in conjunction with treating someone with cancer—is to *boost* the immune system. Doing so gives the person a better chance to survive the cancer and/or subsequent chemotherapy treatments.

The *number-one mistake* people make in fighting over money is focusing on the money. Instead you need to focus on the *relationship* and build it up. Bring it to a point of strength and health, and then you can more easily settle the issue of money. But if you focus on the money, the relationship will eventually tear. It will shred because there's nothing reinforcing it, as you are constantly ripping into each other.

PHASE 1: BUILD UP THE BOND

It helps to spend time together, not talking about the issue at hand. If you can agree to put this issue aside and work on the relationship itself, then either the money problem will resolve itself or your relationship will be in a better shape to withstand the ensuing conflict.

And when you do get together to talk about it, try to do so in a fun, neutral place. Studies show us that anger, being a significant component of conflict, is reduced when we're in an environment that is nonthreatening. And a conversation at the zoo for instance is likely to provoke less anger and animosity than having the conversation over a conference table in the lawyer's office.

If you need to, use techniques in Chapter 27 to get the person to listen to you and spend time with you. Or if there is no contact, write a letter to the person. You will be amazed at how receptive he can be to your reaching out to salvage the relationship.

At this point, with the relationship secured on a more solid foundation, you have two choices. Either seek a mutually agreed upon resolution, or move on to Phase 2 if you feel the situation will have a better outcome if you switch tactics.

PHASE 2: RELINQUISH CONTROL

Tell the person that you believe him to be fair, good, and honest. Tell him that you will leave the decision up to him and you will abide by it. You will often find that *once he has control,* he has no need to assert his power and will probably be fair and balanced in his decision. This is true also because if he's negotiating for something, he wants to get the best deal. "I won" is what he wants to think to himself afterward. But when we're in charge of a situation, we often seek to do what is fair because *there is no psychological gain to getting "more"*—it's up to us anyway. This approach completely locks the ego out of the decision-making process. A conflict is a psychological battle. And as in a physical battle, he doesn't gain anything if, now that he has control, he shoots you in the back.

PHASE 3: DEMONSTRATE TRUST

You want to continue to give this person as much respect and adulation as you can. But simply leaving things up to him, only to convey that you're fearful that he will not do the right thing, will not accomplish your objective. Do not appear concerned. This demonstrates trust. And he will seek to prove that he can be trusted.

Because once the relationship is built up, very often the money issue dissolves. Look at it this way: In what situation can you have one fixed asset where one person uses it but both gain pleasure? Maybe a parent who gives an ice-cream cone to her child. The child enjoys the cone but the parent enjoys the child's pleasure from eating it. If you are in the relationship where there is respect or love or appreciation of the other, then by definition you will be gaining pleasure by giving pleasure.

PHASE 4: SHIFT HIS PERSPECTIVE

As a third party—or with the help of one—use *reframing techniques* so that each sees the situation differently. We usually see things only from our limited perspective and rarely seek to look at things from the other person's point of view. And when we do, it's often skewed. Try to put a positive spin on the reason why each person wants what he does.

> ### OR...
> Maybe the money or asset can go to somebody or to some cause—an event or charity—whom they both would like to have it. In that way they each get to do something nice, and a third party benefits. Another option is to use the asset jointly on something they can both enjoy. Once you do the beginning phases, you will each be in a better place to seek a mutually beneficial resolution—one that keeps the relationship intact.

But alas, we mustn't be naive. If there is no contact or communication and no interest from either side in having any type of relationship, then you don't have a relationship conflict. You have a money conflict. When there is no relationship whatsoever, then use the laws and techniques in Chapter 25, because while this may be a family situation, at this point it is purely business, so you might as well protect your own interests. If money is the objective and not the relationship, the conflict will not be solved without a fight. If money is more important, then *that* becomes the objective. It is a matter of values. What does each person want more?

> ### ONE GREAT SOLUTION
> Write down all the facts both parties agree on. Give the list to ten people who are not familiar with what is going on. Let them read it and decide. This is the fairest and most objective way to conduct your own mini-trial. If each person truly believes he is right, then he will feel comfortable going to a neutral party. You will also very quickly find out who really knows she is being unreasonable. As she fears this method will give her what is fair and not what she claims is fair, she *may* be reluctant to agree.

REAL-WORLD, REAL-LIFE EXAMPLE AND SCENARIO

SCENARIO: Two brothers are fighting over who gets the money from the sale of their grandmother's house. Tim thinks he's entitled to it because he took care of her when she was ill and paid most of her bills. Tom thinks he's entitled to it because, unlike Tim, he really needs the money and would have helped more if he hadn't been working two jobs.

They both agree, with the help of a third party, if necessary, to mutually put the issue of money aside for now and just spend time together talking and doing things unrelated to the situation. Then the one who is in the worst position, in terms of rights to the property, or who wants the relationship more than the money, applies the techniques.

The third-party person, if involved, shows each brother how he can see the situation from the other's perspective and makes them aware of things they might not have been aware of.

"Tim thinks he deserves the money because he spent more than twice that on her medication and nurses."

"Tom is looking to turn things around and wants the money to start a small business. He wants to be able to stand on his own two feet like his big brother, and he sees this as his chance."

[One brother to the other] *"You know what, our relationship means more to me than the money. I will leave it up to you to decide what you want to do."*

He does not then allude to the fact that he is concerned or worried. He continues to treat his brother with respect and love. He will find that his brother, without a battle to fight, becomes more fair.

If you do not meet with the success you want, go to Chapter 28, "In Case of Emergency."

✳ FLASH REVIEW ✳

Whether it's an ongoing argument over who spends how much on what, or it's time to divide up Uncle Harry's estate, when we employ a process that gives each person control and trust while strengthening the relationship itself, money issues take on the proper perspective.

CHAPTER 27

HELP ANYONE GAIN FORGIVENESS: THE PSYCHOLOGICAL
STRATEGY TO GET ONE PERSON TO SIMPLY LISTEN
TO THE OTHER

There are two uses for this chapter. One use is when *you* want to bring
peace between two people and you need to get one to listen to the
other. The second use is when someone *comes to you* and asks for your
help in getting someone to listen to what he has to say—in situations,
for instance, where one person clearly and objectively did something
wrong and the injured party bears very little or none of the blame.
These are cases where one person cheated, stole money, or committed
some other serious violation of trust, confidence, and respect.

BUT, first and foremost, let's be clear: *If he's not sincere, don't inter-
fere.* Make sure you are confident that this person is truly regretful of
his actions and that he is sincere in his wishes to reconcile and make
good on his promise.

STRATEGIC PSYCHOLOGICAL SOLUTION

According to numerous studies and research in human behavior, the following collection of seven psychological rules maximizes your chances of
gaining cooperation in getting one person to listen to the other.

RULE 1: APPROACH HIM WHEN HE'S IN A GOOD MOOD

According to research, people who are in a good mood are more likely
to purchase a lottery ticket. (The reason is that a positive *mood* is sort

of like the shadow of self-esteem, meaning we feel better about ourselves. But this jolt is temporary and not a reflection of our overall psychological well-being.) And when we are in a good mood, we tend to be more *optimistic* to possibilities and receptive to negative information.

You may notice that when you're in a good mood, things don't upset you as much as when you're already upset over something. When you're in a bad mood, even the slightest annoyance can get under your skin. The same holds true for resolving situations. When we're in a good mood we tend to be more open, receptive, and eager to mend fences. The psychology at play is that being in a good mood temporarily boosts self-esteem, which is self-love. This diminishes the ego, and when the ego moves out of the way, our natural desire to connect and relate emerges.

So to use this psychological rule, when he's in an upbeat mood, let him know *clearly* what you want him to do—which is listen to what the other person has to say.

RULE 2: HE'S AT THE CONTROLS

Part of a person's reluctance to hearing someone out is that she feels that once she commits to that, it will be harder for her to "stop the process." As long as she keeps saying no, she is in control. But once she gives in to listening, she loses some of her power. To combat this, you want to convey the following themes:

- She is in complete control. She can leave the conversation whenever she wants—she will not be begged to stay.
- The conversation will be *easy, quick,* and *simple,* not some laborious, painful interaction.
- She doesn't have to commit to anything else. Put her in control, where she does not have to agree to do anything other than just listen. There will be no come-ons or anything to persuade her. You cannot make her think that she will be *sold* on something. She is only there to listen and then decide what she wants to

do—leave, talk, yell, whatever, whatever *she* chooses—*no ifs, ands, or buts*. And make sure that you follow through on this promise.

It is also best to "sandwich" the encounter between two positive experiences. For instance, you would let her know that first you three will meet for lunch, and then after they speak—either with or without you present—you and she will go out to a movie, a concert, or dinner. In this way, she won't be preoccupied on the meeting, and it will also cut down on the chances of her canceling.

THE POLITICIAN'S OUT

Give additional information before you ask him to again reconsider. Nobody wants to be thought of as wishy-washy, meaning that if he changes his mind without any new information he may be perceived, and think of himself, as inconsistent. Rather, before asking him to agree each time, offer some other bit of relevant data or remind him of something he may have forgotten. In this way he can make a new decision based on additional information instead of simply changing his mind

RULE 3: NEGATE HER OWN OBJECTION

Studies show that human beings are driven to act in accordance with how we see ourselves, which is our self-concept. This is also referred to as our "comfort zone," and any action that falls outside of it can make a person uneasy and anxious. More than this, once we make a verbal declaration, meaning that we convey a certain belief to others, our commitment is that much more solidified. Therefore, you would say something such as, "Don't you think that being able to forgive is good for one's mental health?" Or "Don't you think that everyone has a right to at least be heard?" Once she agrees with this statement, she is unconsciously driven to follow through when you ask her to do something that is consistent with this belief that she expressed.

Rule 4: Convey Pain and Remorse

This person needs to understand how the other is suffering—it helps
to reestablish balance. It is important to convey that her misdeeds and
the ensuing loss of the relationship has caused her real pain. If this
person does not believe that the other really cares and is hurting you
will not be successful.

Rule 5: Show That He's a New Person

He must know that the other person not only feels great pain and regret but has also *taken steps to correct the behavior.* This shows that
she's changed. It's not enough for her to feel bad. She must also un-
dergo a kind of transformation to demonstrate that she is different
from what she was. In this way he knows that the relationship he gets
back into will be with a different person and he won't have the same
issue to contend with.

Rule 6: Reshape Self-Concept

We've spoken about the power of this idea in earlier chapters. To use
it here, tell her simply that *you know her to be the kind of person who
is forgiving and open-minded. In fact, that's one of the things you admire most about her.* This statement brings her self-worth and belief
system into the equation. If she were to remain resistant to a reasonable request—in this case to listen to someone who wants to apologize—she would risk having to reevaluate her self-concept.

Rule 7: Dilute Impact

If it is practical and applicable, you want to explain how the other person's actions were not unique to her and were a part of a larger problem. This helps to dilute the impact.

For example, let's say that Joe won't talk to his best friend John, because when John was drunk he cursed him out and pushed him down.
But if Joe discovers that that same night, John also punched the

bouncers at a club and got into two fights on the street, Joe has a slightly different perspective on things. He no longer takes it so personally and is likely to assign John's behavior to something out of the ordinary. With this revised thinking, he's clearly more motivated to listen to what John has to say.

Backup Plan: If you are meeting with intense resistance, try these additional tactics

1. Curiosity Factor. Human beings are driven by a need to satisfy their curiosity. From the celestial heavens to the missing sock in the dryer, we have an insatiable need to know *why.* To use the factor of human curiosity here, if true, you want to let the person know that the reason for the other's actions is something that is remarkable, and that once he hears it, it will put the whole thing into proper perspective. Once you have his curiosity aroused, you tell him the catch is that the other person wants to tell it himself. He will also be moved to find out because *he wants to believe* that there were other circumstances, possibly beyond his control, that might explain the other's actions.

2. What Will It Take? Ask this person what the other needs to do or say in order for him to hear him out. Then, whatever it is, see if the other person can or is willing to agree to his request.

3. Meet in the Middle—Your Middle! If you feel you're going to meet with great resistance, it is best to ask the person to do something way above and beyond the call of duty. For instance, if you have the leverage to do so, insist that she fly across the country and put in all the effort. Then back off from your request and reduce your demands. Now tell her all she has to do *is listen* and you will set everything else up. This will give you solid psychological leverage, as it engages two important laws: *reciprocity* and *contrast.* Essentially, when you back down from your original demand and settle on something less, she will see that you have made concessions and hence will be equally driven to concede. If you just ask her to do something, then she's doing all the work. But when you come down in your demands, she sees it as each of you giving a little. Plus, it engages the *law of contrast,* as the request is not so large when it is seen in light of a larger request.

THE POWER OF PERSISTENCE

Most people say *no* because they are resistant to change. Ask six times. Research shows that across the board most people agree to something after being asked six times. Most people say yes at or before this point if they are going to say yes at all.

REAL-WORLD, REAL-LIFE EXAMPLE AND SCENARIO

Note: Before employing these techniques, satisfy for yourself that this person has changed and that he is truly remorseful. Most important, be sure that a reconciliation is in the best interests of *both* parties.

SCENARIO: A friend cheated on his wife and has come to you for help. You know his wife, too, and she says that she just wants a divorce and won't listen to anything he has to say. Clearly, he knows what he did was wrong, he regrets it, and he thoroughly believes that if he could just talk to her—using the technique in Chapter 17—that she will forgive him.

First you lay the groundwork a day or so ahead of time.

> *"Do you think forgiveness is important?"* or *"How much of our happiness in life depends upon sealing old wounds?"*

You bring up a question like this so that she begins to solidify in her mind that this is the kind of person she is. This is followed by a statement such as, *"That's one of the things that I've always respected about you."* Or *"I've always admired people who aren't afraid to take a chance."*

This does two things: it reshapes her self-concept to include the definition of someone who believes in this, and it prevents her own objection later, as she has already stated that it is important to forgive.

Then approach her about the subject when she's in a good mood, or excited or looking forward to something:

"I was speaking with Hal and he is just devastated at what he did. He's barely been eating. You should know that he's been in counseling ever since—two days a week for now—and he's hoping to increase that so he can beat this problem as soon as possible."

Keep selling—repeating and emphasizing—these points:

- *"I just want you to listen to what he has to say. When he's done explaining, that's it. He won't try to sway you. You don't even have to forgive him. I just want you to hear what he has to say directly from him and I think it will help you to completely understand what happened.*
- *"It's simple. You and I will have dinner at my house. He'll come over, you'll talk, and then he'll go. That's it. And afterward you and I can grab a movie."*
- *"He's in so much pain. I know that you are, too. But it may be that what he has to say will help you. Because he said that there is something that you are unaware of. And he wants to tell you himself. I think it will help you to be at peace with it. Even if you don't want anything to do with him, do it for you."*

These ideas will begin to get through as long as you sincerely have both people's interest at heart. It is not good for her to hold on to anger. Just the conversation, even if she doesn't choose to forgive him, will help her to have closure.

If you do not meet with the success you want, go to Chapter 28, "In Case of Emergency."

✳ FLASH REVIEW ✳

When you want to get one person to hear another out, a seven-rule system will give you all the psychological firepower you need. According to studies, negating the person's own objection, reshaping the self-concept, diluting his intentions, and providing an alternate motivation will give you the leverage to accomplish your objective.

CHAPTER 28

In Case of Emergency:

Seven Advanced Psychological Tactics for the Most
Stubborn, Difficult, and Trying People and Situations

!!!!!
IN CASE OF EMERGENCY

These tactics are used when nothing else is working. Only you, knowing the situation and person(s) involved, can know best which to use.
Many can be used consecutively in any order that is needed, while
some may negate the use of others.

These techniques should be used by a *third party only*—preferably,
someone who is neutral and not directly involved in the conflict. The
reason is that these techniques can be viewed as psychologically inva-
sive. They must be engaged in by someone who has nothing but an al-
truistic motivation.

Once you engage these techniques, either employ or reemploy your
psychological strategy in the appropriate chapter.

EMERGENCY TACTIC 1: A DOSE OF REALITY

Have you ever driven by a bad traffic accident and noticed that the
people you're in the car with suddenly become *nicer* to one another?
There's a sort of quiet kindness that permeates. Have you ever been to
visit a friend at the hospital and the second you walk out the lobby
doors you look around and see the world just a little bit differently?
You feel a mix of relief, sadness, and optimism. In essence, the experience produces a *shift in perspective*. You feel *happy to be alive and*

grateful for what you have. These situations give us a healthy dose of perspective, but it too soon wears off.

For one or both parties to experience this psychological shift, take each one, always separately—to the hospital, a funeral home, or whatever—to jolt them back into reality. You want them to see what in life is really important and what really matters. Many people seem to connect on this spiritual level, more than on the logical or emotional level—and it is often highly effective.

This works so well for us because we are looking at everything—including people and situations—with more kindness and empathy and with a healthier perspective. And this change in our perspective gives us the opportune time to patch things up. You want to strike while the iron is hot! Have them commit then and there to meeting/talking on a set date as soon as possible.

EMERGENCY TACTIC 2: YOUR SWAN SONG

If you've suffered some sort of recent tragedy or hardship—for example, your house burned down, you were diagnosed with an illness, or your dog died—then someone wanting to help you feel better and not add to your pain will also be more likely to acquiesce to what it is that you want. Additionally, he can see that if you are asking for this with all that has just happened to you, then *it must be important* to you and he will not want to disappoint you further.

That said, even if the "tragedy" is not so great, it really doesn't matter, because it is just the psychological motivation that the person needs. Emphasize, simply, that he is not doing it for the other person or even for himself *but for you.* Even if you don't think that you have enough clout, it probably won't matter, because most people just need a psychological excuse to remove their ego from the equation. As long as the person feels he is doing it *for you,* it eliminates much of his baggage.

It can be hard to understand this idea. Because our ego is a piece of our own puzzle, we often can't see objectively what an action *independent* of our ego looks like. Let's say that you're a single person who went out by yourself to a singles bar. You might feel a little self-conscious. But now let's say that you were heading up a research project on the social interaction of *men with gold chains and bad pickup lines and the women who love them.* Now when you go, you're not self-conscious, because *it's not about you,* it's about them and your job. You're ego isn't on the line. In much the same way, making peace between two people involves, some of the time, *removing them* and making it about someone or something else.

Make it about what *you want and need.* And go for the highest level of interaction—whether it's a short talk, one listening to the other, the two of them working together on a project, or outright reconciliation.

EMERGENCY TACTIC 3: THE REALITY CHECK

When all else fails . . . *scare the person.* We think that we have an infinite amount of time—that when we get around to it, we'll always have a chance to talk and work things out if we choose to. But the reality is, of course, *we don't,* and we never know what tomorrow will bring. Since fear is what is keeping the two people from connecting, then use fear to help you melt away the conflict.

For instance, you would say something like, "I have some sad news. I want to talk to you about your sister." He will, of course, think the worst—that she's been hurt or killed. Don't say anything else until he speaks, and then say how much this rift is hurting her. This jolts them into the reality of life and out of this fantasy that we have an infinite amount of time and that tomorrow is guaranteed to us. Will they be upset that you did this? Probably insanely angry. But once they have reconciled, they will be grateful for you doing what you had to do to bring them back together.

You won't have as much of a mess as you might suspect. The more upset this person is at you, the more it means that he cares and wants to reconcile conflict. Therefore, clarify for him the need and value in establishing peace.

EMERGENCY TACTIC 4: THE UNIVERSE IS SENDING ME A MESSAGE

This is the kind of psychological technique that can work on the most stubborn of people. When someone refuses to listen to you or others, there is one source or entity that he will listen to: Call it God, the universe, a higher power, karmic law, whatever. At any rate, if he feels that the *universe* is trying to tell him something, then he may listen. He won't listen to you or anyone else, but the universe, that's a different story.

So, for instance, ask him to be on the lookout for signs that the universe is trying to give him a message that he should reconcile/apologize/listen. Now, if he unconsciously or consciously wants to do this, this will give him the psychological permission that he needs, and he will begin to see signs.

To illustrate how this works, let's take an example from your own life. Have you ever had the experience of buying a new car only to begin to notice that everyone was driving the same car you were? Or were you ever thinking about an old friend and then kept running into people that looked like him? The same is true here. If he looks, he will find. And as long as he believes that it is coming from "the universe" and not from a mere mortal, he will be moved to respond.

EMERGENCY TACTIC 5: I NEVER KNEW

Our focus is our reality. What we choose to focus on becomes our world. It produces our thoughts, values, attitudes, and beliefs. If you want to help two people reestablish ties, then shift the focus of how each sees the other. For example, if one person has done something extremely remarkable—such as saved a life, donated a kidney, or adopted a child—it may dramatically change how the other sees him. This creates a psychological ripple effect whereby he is forced—at mostly an unconscious level—to reevaluate his opinion and attitude toward the other person.

We can find reasons to dislike anyone. But it's what you focus on and appreciate in a person that cultivates a positive relationship.

EMERGENCY TACTIC 6: IT'S TOO LATE FOR ME, BUT NOT FOR YOU

Unfortunately, there is no shortage of people who would give their life savings to have a five-minute conversation with someone who has passed on.

Ask one of these people who never had the chance to reconcile with someone in her life to speak to one or both of those involved in *your* conflict. The guilt and self-destructiveness caused by not being able to make things right can be enormous. Therefore, you will be doing *all* the people involved a great favor. Even for the person who has lost her chance, explaining and conveying to someone else the importance of forgiving will often help alleviate much of her own guilt and suffering. *This is a very powerful tool in getting one person to at least hear the other out.*

EMERGENCY TACTIC 7: RESHUFFLING THE DECK

Use any significant event in either of their lives as an on-ramp to peace. Positive or negative; whether it's a birth or a death, events like these cause the psychological deck to be reshuffled. And you'll have a better chance at drawing a new hand. Meaning that how we see things, our values, our perspective, and our priorities get realigned. This provides the perfect opportunity to just get the ball rolling and open the communication gateway.

Any action—a phone call, card, or gift—to acknowledge any illness, crisis, award, and so on, is one of the simplest and most powerful methods to accelerate and establish a reconciliation.

CHAPTER 29

Regardless of the dynamics, whether it's a relationship with a friend, family, or coworker, you can significantly enhance your relations by following nine incredibly simple rules, and with very little effort on your part. These rules are elementary, yet they lie at the foundation of every relationship.

RULE 1: SHOW GENUINE ENTHUSIASM WHEN YOU GREET THE PERSON

The power of this rule is astounding. If you, upon seeing her, walk over with a big smile and a genuine sign of pleasure for being with her, you will make her feel like a million dollars. She will, in turn, show vast appreciation for your making her feel so comfortable, welcomed, and regarded.

RULE 2: SHOW RESPECT

This means not criticizing the person harshly, and certainly never in front of anyone else. Do not roll your eyes or make any gesture that shows a lack of respect. This also means you show reverence when you are *not* with this person by not gossiping or speaking poorly about her to anyone else. And when she's speaking to you, give her your *full attention;* do not read or have your focus divided. These are such little things, but they impact greatly on how two people get along.

RULE 3: BE SUPPORTIVE

When she makes a mistake, let her know that it's something anyone could have done and that she shouldn't be so hard on herself. Do not be quick to criticize and condemn. She will only get defensive and argumentative. By being supportive when she is down, you show that you care about her and not simply your own interests. Be on *her* side. There is no merit or reward for being right, or in proving that you are smarter than she is. You don't gain anything. There is, however, reward for showing compassion and support—a terrific relationship.

RULE 4: GIVE HER THE BENEFIT OF THE DOUBT

Learn to judge favorably when she does something that appears to be a reflection of a lack of respect for you. If she keeps you waiting or takes something without permission, assume that she had a good reason. And if you inquire about it, don't be accusatory and argumentative. Even if her motivation was less than pure, your actions this time will change hers the next time.

RULE 5: LET HER KNOW YOU APPRECIATE HER

It's amazing, but it seems that in all kinds of relationships, the only time we say something nice is when we've done something wrong. Be proactive from time to time. One nice word in the bank is worth a hundred after the fact.

RULE 6: GIVE HER THE CHANCE TO CONTRIBUTE TO YOUR LIFE

There is no greater way to bond with someone than letting her be a part of you and invest herself in you. Ask this person for advice, and for input, whenever you think she might have something worthwhile to contribute. Allowing her to give makes her feel good and brings you both closer.

RULE 7: WAIT TWENTY-FOUR HOURS IF THE PERSON DOES SOMETHING THAT ANGERS YOU

You'll be amazed at how your perspective shifts in that short period of time. Indeed, if you still feel the need to mention it, your approach will be more balanced and objective.

RULE 8: TALK ABOUT WHAT IS BOTHERING YOU

When something is bothering you, or the other person's actions frustrate or annoy you, bring it up. Talk to him about it so it doesn't fester and cause a more serious problem. Keeping things inside is rarely good for the relationship or you. But be tactful. And bear in mind that you do not want to nitpick at every little thing. Only bring out issues that are truly troubling.

RULE 9: SHARE YOURSELF AND OPEN UP A BIT WITH THIS PERSON

Even if it's not a personal relationship, let this person into your life a bit. While some people are by nature very expressive, many of us are more closed. If you're this type of reserved person, you may find this tactic greatly enhances your relationship.

Once there is shared mutual respect, then most any minor transgression or oversight by either person is filtered through this new lens. Any misunderstanding or miscommunication is viewed as an honest, unintentional mistake.

FREQUENTLY ASKED QUESTIONS

QUESTIONS THAT MAY BE ON YOUR MIND

Q What if the other person doesn't want peace? What do I do with a person who simply doesn't care about mending fences? Should I even try?

A The short answer is that you should always try. You never know. And it is your obligation to attempt a reconciliation. Think for a moment about the reason why you would not even try to make things right. You might look foolish, waste your time, be embarrassed, you've already given so much, and so on. All of these expressions are tied into the ego.

If someone offered you a million dollars and you'd do it then, then do it now. Not trying is the only thing you may regret. Everyone *wants* to have good, positive relationships, but it's our fears and hangups that get in the way. So even if he says he does not want to end the conflict, often that is just hurt and pain talking. Think of a child who tells her mother that she hates her because she won't let her have ice cream for breakfast. The child is simply lashing out, and we adults act similarly when we are angry.

Q How many times and for how long should I try ?

A Of course you shouldn't bang your head against the wall. If, after several times of trying over a period of time, you meet with great resistance, then it might be best to move on. The quality of any relationship is determined by the one who wants it least, not most. But understand that there is a difference between someone not *wanting* to forgive and someone who is *uninterested* in having any type of relationship or friendship. So if the other person—or both people, if you are acting as a third party—have no interest in reconciling, then definitely move on. If it's a case, however, where the hurt or pain is just too intense for this person to move past it now, then I would encourage you to revisit the situation after a few months—or a year, depending on what happened—and to try again. Because in this instance, it is the pain and not the lack of desire to reconcile that is keeping them apart.

Q Some of these techniques seem manipulative. Is it okay to lie to make peace?

A Decide what you want and what is important. Manipulation is about getting someone to ignore reality and instead listen to you. But you are bringing reality to a person or people who are in the land of illusion.

If you want to use the Bible as a barometer for morality, then it is clear that lying to keep or maintain peace *is allowable.* But with that said, it is allowable only when completely necessary and as seldom as possible, only as needed to accomplish your objective. And if you want to use common sense, then ask yourself why it is wrong to lie. It is wrong, of course, because someone is usually injured by the deception. But here you are using tactics to bring people together, only for the benefit of each other. There is nothing selfish whatsoever.

Q What about patterns of conflicts? What if the reason for the conflict has to do with deeper psychologically based motivations, such as something from childhood?

A People get into negative patterns of relationships for one or a combination of three reasons.

1. They are looking to seal a wound from the past. Simply, if a woman was abused as a small child, then she may find herself in a cycle of abusive relationships as a way to unconsciously *correct* the mistake. Meaning that she is seeking to right the wrongs of the past by changing how things unfold now. And to

do this, she attracts situations that allow her to relive the scenario time and again.

2. The second reason is that some people are unconsciously driven out of guilt or self-anger to set themselves up in these conflicts in order to "get back at themselves." They unconsciously engage in these negative patterns because they feel that is all that they are worthy of.

3. Finally, sometimes we engage in a pattern of conflict because we have a belief about how the world should be and a self-concept that supports it. Therefore, we unconsciously seek events and dynamics that will unfold exactly the way we expect they should. This is why people with certain character traits, such as anger, are drawn to other angry people. This is how they see their world, and so they bring people and situations into it to conform to their expectations of reality.

The reason the psychological strategies are so effective is that regardless of the underlying motivation behind the patterns of conflict, these types of people are all ultimately seeking what we give them: a sense of self-worth and independence. That is, a feeling that they are in control. We restore their sense of power over what happens in their life.

Q What about different personality types?

A We all see the world just a little bit differently. Some of us process our experiences through a logical filter, while others are more emotionally oriented. And of course some people are more kinesthetic, some visual, and others auditory. We have the introvert and the extrovert. But no matter which model you use there is a common thread, one that we amplify and address, and that is respect.

We all want to be *validated*, regardless of our perception. These techniques transcend personality, patterns of behavior, even mild mental illness. They go to the root of the psyche and repair the damage. You don't have to spend months or even years getting through any of these filters or trying to learn how the other person sees his or her world. Fundamentally, we all crave and need the same psychological nourishment. This is why the strategies are as effective as they are and work as quickly as they do. They are fundamentals of human nature and human behavior, going beneath the surface of personality.

Q What if he's a real jerk?

A You are not obligated to have someone in your life who causes you pain. If someone does nothing but drain you emotionally, or is harmful and hurtful, then you shouldn't want that person in your life. That said, be sure that the reason he behaves this way to you isn't simply that he feels you are not giving him the respect he needs. So try the techniques first. Besides, you can end a conflict, put the past behind you, and still want nothing to do with the person. This is okay. And if someone keeps doing something objectionable to you—same actions and same apology without any new steps—then call it a day. Someone who is sincere will not only apologize verbally but will also take steps to best ensure that he does not repeat his mistake. Additionally, he should take whatever reasonable steps are necessary to correct the damage done.

Q What if *I* want to be forgiven but I'm not sure that I won't do the same thing again?

A *Then don't ask for forgiveness.* Part of the process is regretting your actions and resolving not to repeat your behavior. If you want to be a good, responsible human being, then work on yourself before you work on the relationship.

Q Why can't I be angry about something that was blatantly abusive?

A While we may think someone is "out of line" or behaved wrongly, understand that *every bit of anger and negative emotion is tied into our ego.* Now, there is no one alive who does not, to some degree, have an ego. We all do. But understand that, theoretically, if you had complete *one hundred percent total self-love,* you would never be of-

fended, hurt, or embarrassed in any situation. (I use this example because sometimes it is easier to see things in the extreme.) We cloak
ourselves in these emotions to protect our fragile ego. This is hard to
conceive of, but I assure you, as I've assured you elsewhere in this
book, it is where there is a tear in our esteem that the ego breaks
through. It is the ego that becomes angered.

Remember earlier we talked about loss of control as being the basis
of anger? Well, as we saw, self-esteem is *precisely* what gives us the
feeling of being in control. And again, theoretically speaking, with
complete esteem comes total control and hence a person can never, by
definition, become angry, since anger finds its root in fear, which finds
its root in loss of control.

We experience an emotional pain—from being out of control—and
that pain turns into anger. At the root of all anger lies one underlying
emotion: *fear. Period.* It is the extension of fear that causes feuds and
conflict and disagreements. So make sure your assessment is not emotionally charged and you are looking at the person and the situation
objectively and logically.

While you may want nothing to do with this person, anger is not a
response that will allow you to deal with him, the situation, and yourself responsibly, with clarity and objectivity.

Q Why is it that some people simply don't get it? They seem to have
such a warped perspective on people and life in general.

A Self-esteem gives us *perspective* on situations and relationships.
It determines what gets placed in the "it matters" or the "it doesn't
matter" category. How important something is to you determines the
degree that you are sensitive to it. That said, higher esteem gives us
greater perspective on what is really important, and things are perceived and understood with greater objectivity.

The lower a person's self-esteem, the greater the impact that minor events have. She is focused on the here and now, like a child—she
has a narrowed perspective—just as if she were a young girl playing
with a doll who suddenly finds it snatched away by her brother. To her,
her whole world has been disrupted. Low self-esteem causes us to lose

sight of the larger picture. The person with low self-esteem will "freak out" upon discovering a scratch on the dining room floor, while someone with greater self-esteem recognizes that this is not the end of the world. This is why many of the techniques we use snap a person into the true reality, where everything else—the silliness, the unimportant things—fades away.

Q If a relationship is not working, doesn't it take two to change?

A The answer is yes and no. If you change how you relate to someone, then that person is no longer relating to the same person. You've changed his behavior merely by changing yours. Many of the strategies effect change in this way. When the dynamics of the relationship change by the behavior of just one person, it produces a change in the other. Your power to cause a dramatic transformation in another is enormous simply by modifying how you *relate* to that person.

Q What if this person wants absolutely nothing to do with me?

A He may have a very good reason. That said, if he does not have a complete picture or is not privy to all the facts, in addition to the techniques in Chapter 28, "In Case of Emergency," you may find *indirect communication* to be highly effective. Using the psychological strategies specific to your situation, you can write letters and use tapes to express your feelings. Persistence and sincerity are two powerful allies, and your efforts, no matter how daunting the situation, can pay off if you are determined.

CONCLUSION

In my book *Never Be Lied to Again,* I wrote that honesty is the cornerstone of every relationship. We might appropriately add here that relationships are the cornerstone of our lives.

We are not always able to choose who comes in and out of our lives, but now perhaps you are better able to make those relationships as rewarding and as special as you choose.

And remember, relationships are built on trust, respect, and honesty. To ensure that you're able to reestablish peace quickly and effectively, please observe the guidelines in the section "A Note to Readers."

I wish you very good relationships and a very good life.

THE POWER OF PERSISTENCE

What this power is I cannot say; all I know is that it exists and it becomes available only when a man is in that state of mind in which he knows exactly what he wants and is fully determined not to quit until he finds it.

—ALEXANDER GRAHAM BELL

I do not think there is any quality so essential to success of any kind as the quality of perseverance. It overcomes almost everything, even nature.

—JOHN D. ROCKEFELLER

When I have fully decided that a result is worth getting, I go ahead on it and make trial after trial until it comes.

—THOMAS EDISON

ABOUT THE AUTHOR

David J. Lieberman, Ph.D., whose books have been translated into fifteen languages, is an internationally renowned leader in the field of human behavior. He has appeared on more than two hundred programs and is a frequent guest expert on national television and radio shows such as *The Today Show,* National Public Radio, *The View,* PBS, *The Montel Williams Show,* and A&E. Dr. Lieberman holds a Ph.D. in psychology and is the creator of Neural-Dynamic Analysis, a revolutionary short-term therapy. He is a sought-after speaker, lecturer, and consultant across a spectrum of fields. Techniques based on his work have led to groundbreaking advancements in numerous areas and are used by governments, corporations, and professionals in more than twenty-five countries. He lives in New York City and Florida.

Dr. Lieberman offers special programs, training, and workshops in the United States and throughout the world. Please send your request for information to the following address or visit us at our Web site.

Lieberman & Associates
P.O. Box 810775
Boca Raton, FL 33481

www.makepeacewithanyone.com